Contents

Figures and Tables

Figures

Tables

Foreword

Making a sale is the central driving force of all business. The nature of the sale, its complexity, its size, and the development time and effort involved may vary enormously from one business to another and from one particular situation to another. The salesperson may not act alone—and usually does not, in fact. The sale is normally the result of a marketing process, the purpose of which is to create favorable conditions for a sale. Although some sales are transacted through an impersonal process such as mail-order catalogues, the final common element for all personal selling is a salesperson who "makes the sale."

Because sales are the ultimate measure of business performance, and because a salesperson is necessary for a sale to be made, it is surprising that research-based literature on the performance of salespeople and on the selling process has been scanty and scattered. In contrast, such fields of advertising, new product development, and measurement techniques have produced a rich literature. Fortunately, as the authors point out, there has been a steady increase in the number and quality of studies conducted during the past ten to fifteen years. However, these new studies and the existing sources within the literature have not until now been integrated in a way that can be most useful as a knowledge-base for industry practitioners and university teachers.

Happily for both industry and academe, Professor James Comer and Professor Alan Dubinsky have made an important contribution by synthesizing the literature on sales management in *Managing the Successful Sales Force*. They have selected research evidence on the considerations that are most important to sales managers—recruiting, selecting, and managing sales personnel—and they have organized this evidence in a way that can be most useful for sales managers by describing what the research found and what the research suggests.

It is a continuing goal of the Marketing Science Institute to encourage and support research that will advance marketing knowledge and increase marketing productivity. It is gratifying, therefore, that the MSI has played a supportive role in helping to forward the original idea proposed by Professor Comer to the final point of publication.

Alden G. Clayton
Marketing Science Institute

Preface

This book is primarily for the practicing manager seeking guidance in the recruitment, selection, and management of sales personnel. It shows how research results can be translated into day-to-day operating decisions. The text should also be of interest to researchers and teachers in the field of sales management who want a synthesis of prior research on sales force management.

We wish to thank academic researchers for their efforts, which made this work possible, and also the Marketing Science Institute, who initially funded this study. Diane Schmalensee, Director of Research Operations for the Marketing Science Institute, was particularly helpful in the early preparation of the text. We also wish to thank the following individuals for their dedicated and expert assistance: Ms. Donna Meyer, Ms. Diane Hammond, Ms. Debra A. Cusick, and Ms. Lisa Snyder. Obviously, all errors of omission and commission reside with the authors.

1
Introduction

P ersonal selling is the driving force behind many marketing organizations today. The old adage "Nothing moves until the sale is made" is very true. For example, without a competent and effective sales force, manufacturing facilities may be underutilized, support personnel may engage in "make-work" tasks, potentially salable products or services may remain unsold, and company viability could be placed in jeopardy. The importance of personal selling and salesmanship to the company was defined as long ago as 1918:

> What the sun is to the earth salesmanship [personal selling] is to business. Without the creative power of the sun . . . the earth would become a desolate wilderness. . . . Salesmanship is the force that keeps business moving. . . . Salesmanship is the creator of happiness, the bulwark of continued efficient service to humanity. Without the creative force of salesmanship, the greatest inventions would have rusted away without ever reaching the user. . . . Salesmanship is the driving wheel of commerce. The individual salesman is a cog in the wheel that keeps business moving. (*The Art and Science of Selling,* 1918, p. 9)

To realize the potential of their sales personnel, sales managers engage in several critical activities. Figure 1–1 illustrates the major duties of most sales managers. As shown in this figure, sales managers are responsible for three key functions: planning, implementation, and control. *Planning* involves adopting a future-oriented perspective (Where do we want to go?) and is concerned with organizing the sales force (e.g., by territory, product, or customer), forecasting sales volume, establishing budgets, setting quotas, and designing sales territories. *Implementation* involves developing means with which to achieve the sales plans (How will we attain our goals?). Implementation activities include recruitment and selection of salespeople, development and execution of sales training programs, establishment of adequate compensation and expense programs, design of nonfinancial motivational programs, and supervision. *Control* entails evaluation of sales department

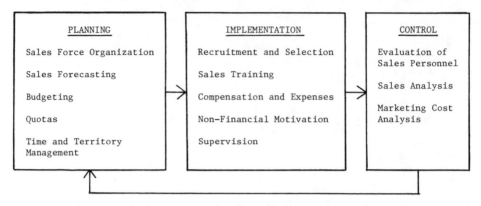

Figure 1–1. Activities of Sales Managers

performance (Did we achieve our goals or meet our plans?). Particular attention is given to assessing each salesperson's performance and conducting sales and marketing cost analyses (profitability analyses). For a detailed discussion of each of these sales management functions, see a current sales management text such as Churchill, Ford, and Walker (1981).

These management activities have generally been practiced by using a combination of intuition, company or industry tradition, or other nonempirical approaches. This is not to say that managers have ignored the results of empirical research or that researchers have failed to explore sales management issues. On the contrary, researchers, particularly within the past twenty years, have conducted extensive research focusing on the management of salespeople. To date, however, few attempts have been made to review systematically this previous empirical work *and* to provide sales managers with a practical interpretation of the findings of this prior research. Consequently, sales managers' use of published findings probably has been limited.

Purpose of the Book

This book is intended to present results of previous research and to offer pragmatic conclusions from these results in two broad areas of sales management: (1) recruitment and selection of sales personnel, and (2) management of sales personnel. The sales management literature reviewed encompasses the period from 1923 to mid-1984, and the majority of substantive work has been conducted within the past fifteen years. Only studies employing empirical data that were subjected to generally accepted data analysis procedures were included in the review. Research that concentrated on case histories of companies was not included. Also excluded were investigations of methodology, comparative criticisms, or proposition development. No assessment was made of a study's methodology, nor of its choice or development of instrumentation. Study dimensions, therefore, are reported as they were detailed by the original researchers.

By way of definition, the term "manager" in the book refers to the first-line sales supervisor (or field sales manager). The term "salesperson" denotes a member of the field sales force who is an employee and is under the control of a manager.

Organization of the Book

This book is divided into two major sections. Part I contains four chapters describing research that focused on recruitment and selection of sales personnel in terms of selected variables that may predict sales success (e.g., age, height, and educational level). Specifically, chapter 2 presents studies that examined predictors of sales success in consumer product and service selling; chapter 3, industrial product and service selling; chapter 4, life insurance selling; and chapter 5, retail selling.

Part II contains three chapters reviewing empirical work that examined issues related to management of sales personnel. Chapter 6 discusses findings of studies investigating means of enhancing salespeople's motivation, resolving their job conflicts, and clarifying their job tasks and responsibilities. Chapter 7 presents findings of research that has explored salesperson job satisfaction. Chapter 8 focuses on the all-important issue of salesperson job performance and the research on this topic. The book concludes with a postscript that contains a summary of the implications of the material reviewed.

Technical terms are not defined in the text. Rather, their definitions can be found in the easy-to-use glossary, which appears after the postscript. To maintain simplicity in the discussion, descriptions of the studies' methodologies, data analysis procedures, and numeric results are not reported in the chapters; instead, this information is presented in tabular form in the appendix.

Part I
Recruitment and Selection of Sales Personnel

The recruitment and selection process is a key sales management function. The marketing folklore is replete with anecdotes about individuals assuming sales positions for which they were unqualified and about the ramifications of such hiring decisions (e.g., miffed customers, inefficient use of company resources, and missed performance targets). Moreover, recruiting sales personnel is a costly activity. American firms spend in excess of $5 billion annually to recruit and train salespeople hired to replace those who have left (Weitz 1979). This estimate, however, includes only direct costs and ignores the all-important indirect costs such as:

Disproportionate sales management time allocated to dealing with terminated salespeople and their replacements;

Actual lost sales from customers not called on or managed improperly;

New business never acquired;

Loss of customer confidence.

Given the significance of correct hiring decisions, it is vital for sales managers to be able to identify characteristics (variables) of individuals that are related to sales success. It would be particularly useful to be able to identify observable and/or testable variables that discriminate between sales and non-sales personnel and low-performing and high-performing salespeople; and it would be especially relevant to be able to determine the relative amounts or combinations of these variables that are present in a sales recruit *prior* to selecting the recruit. Identification of such variables would help sales managers determine which candidates to hire.

Researchers, particularly within the past thirty years, have attempted to identify variables that predict how successful a sales recruit might be. Results of these investigations, however, have been mixed (Churchill, Ford, and Walker 1981; Weitz 1979). This inconsistency in results is partly because researchers have examined different types of selling situations (e.g., industrial, consumer, and retail selling) and employed many methods of measurement. The inconsistencies may also be due to inappropriate classification schemes used by evaluators to compare results across studies. Thus, an approach that systematically categorizes the results of previous studies into meaningful groups (such as by type of selling) and then examines the findings relevant to each group may produce insights directly useful to sales managers in those and similar areas. The purpose of this kind of classification schema is to classify similar activities, objects, and/or events so as to simplify analysis and understanding of the research results.

For ease of interpretation, the studies reviewed in Part I are classified into four groups, based upon the nature of the samples (e.g., consumer and industrial) employed in the studies. The four categories are: consumer product and service sales, industrial product and service sales, insurance sales, and retail sales. The former two kinds of selling are distinguished in this book because the marketing literature has traditionally viewed industrial and consumer marketing as distinct entities. The latter two kinds of selling are examined separately because perusal of the previous studies indicated that insurance and retail selling have a large enough number of studies to justify their own categories.

Prior investigations exploring the factors or characteristics predicting success in sales have typically examined one or more variables in four categories. As shown in figure I–1, the four sets of variables are: physical traits, mental abilities, personality characteristics, and experience/background factors (Churchill, Ford, and Walker 1981).

Physical traits include observable characteristics such as a person's age, sex, height, physical attractiveness, and similarity to a customer. (Although

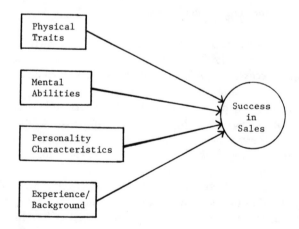

Figure 1–1. Potential Predictors of Success in Sales

discussed in Part I, certain physical traits—such as age and sex—must be used with caution in the recruiting process because of federal guidelines that state that a firm's selection criteria must be related to job performance and cannot discriminate on the basis of age, sex, race, and so on.)

Mental abilities are an individual's cognitive capacity and are assessed by tests of intelligence, mathematical ability, verbal ability, and the like.

Personality characteristics entail inherent features of an individual that can be generalized into two major categories: sociability (which includes extroversion, adaptability, identification, empathy, and so on), and forcefulness (which includes dominance, ego drive, self-confidence/assurance, aggressiveness, and the like).

Experience/background factors encompass such variables as education, family background, leadership experience, job experience, and previous responsibilities.

The discussions of the results of previous research within each selling category will be grouped according to these four sets of variables. When presenting these results, the term *success* is used broadly. Although previous researchers have defined success in a variety of ways (such as self- or manager-ratings of performance, sales volume, or percent of quota), for convenience the general term *success* is employed rather than such multiple measures.

2
Consumer Product and Service Sales

T his chapter presents results and implications of studies focusing on identification of variables that predict success in selling consumer products or services (see appendix, table A–1). Consumer product or service salespeople sell products or services that are used by the ultimate consumer, but the actual sale might be to either resellers (wholesalers or retailers) or consumers. In the investigations reviewed here, salespeople marketed such offerings as automobiles, petroleum-related products, stocks and bonds, food, hardware, appliances, and real estate. Research results reviewed in this chapter are based upon thirteen different works from the personal selling and sales management literature.

What the Research Found

Physical Characteristics

None of the thirteen works reviewed focused on physical characteristics that may predict success in consumer selling.

Mental Abilities

Several studies have examined relationships between mental abilities and consumer selling success. Intelligence—both general and social—has generally been shown to be positively correlated with sales success (Ghiselli 1969, 1973; Harrell 1960; Mattheiss et al. 1974). That is, the higher their level of intelligence, the more successful sales personnel tend to be in the job. In addition, oral arithmetic ability (Miner 1962) and mental ability (Harrell 1960) have been found to be positively associated with sales success.

Some investigations demonstrate, however, that the nature of the consumer sales job may mediate the relationship between intelligence and sales success. Austin (1954) reviewed thirty research studies (conducted between

1915 and 1950) that examined the relationship between intelligence and sales success. His review led to the following conclusions:

> There is a small inverse relationship between salesperson intelligence and sales ability for salespeople in "lower" grades of selling. In other words, there is a slight tendency for people with lower levels of intelligence in low-level sales positions to perform better than their counterparts with higher levels of intelligence.
>
> Intelligence appears to be unrelated to sales success for salespeople in jobs of an "average" grade.
>
> Intelligence is positively related to sales success for salespersons in "high" grade sales positions. Thus, the higher the level of one's intelligence, the greater degree of salesperson success in these kinds of jobs.

When evaluating Austin's (1954) conclusions, however, caution should be exercised because he did not carefully distinguish among the criteria for "low," "average," and "high" grade selling jobs, nor did he clearly specify the kind of intelligence measured.

Personality Characteristics

The relationship between personality characteristics and success in consumer selling has been a topic of great interest in the research field. A variety of personality characteristics that fall under the sociability/forcefulness dichotomy have been examined in this research.

Sociability. Empathy appears to be positively related to sales success (Greenberg and Mayer 1964; Mayer and Greenberg 1964; Tobolski and Kerr 1952). Furthermore, Greenberg and Mayer (1964) indicated that empathy measures can successfully predict high-performing sales personnel over time. Miner (1962) discovered that sociophilia and happiness were positively correlated with sales success, but that higher levels of sociophobia were related to low sales performance.

A salesperson's social orientation—extroverted versus introverted—has also been shown to be related to sales success. Extroversion appears to be positively associated with sales success, particularly when the salesperson exhibits high ego involvement (Howells 1968). In addition, a sense of humor has been determined to be positively correlated with manager's rating of salesperson success but unrelated to sales volume (Harrell 1960). Scheibelhut and Albaum (1973) discovered that higher levels of complexity (complex persons are more likely to see similarities between themselves and others) were positively related to sales success.

Several measures of salesperson sociability appear to be unrelated to sales success. Social interest, self centrality, and inclusion were found by Scheibel-hut and Albaum (1973), and sociometric popularity by Mattheiss et al. (1974), to be unrelated to sales success.

Forcefulness. Findings on the relationships between measures of forcefulness and success in consumer selling are somewhat inconsistent. For example, although Scheibelhut and Albaum (1973) found self esteem to be unrelated to sales success, self assurance and self confidence were determined to be positively correlated with sales success by Ghiselli (1969), Harrell (1960), and Miner (1962), but not by Mattheiss et al. (1974). In addition, aggressiveness and drive were positively associated with sales success (Greenberg and Mayer 1964; Harrell 1960); conversely, low levels of aggressiveness have been associated with low levels of performance (Miner 1962). However, Baehr and Williams (1968) discovered that drive was correlated with only one of four success variables. Dominance has been positively related to sales volume (Harrell 1960) and managerial rating of performance (Dunnette and Kirchner 1960), but also has been shown as unrelated to managerial rating of performance (Harrell 1960). Aspiration level (desire to be a sales manager) was found to be both positively correlated (Dunnette and Kirchner 1960; Harrell 1960) and negatively correlated (Mattheiss et al. 1974) with sales success. Ego drive appears to be positively associated with sales success (Greenberg and Mayer 1964; Mayer and Greenberg 1964) and can successfully predict high-performing sales personnel over time (Greenberg and Mayer 1964).

Experience/Background

Only one study was found that focused on salesperson experience/background factors as predictors of success in consumer selling. Baehr and Williams (1968) discovered the following:

Responsibility (as measured by financial and early family background) was positively correlated with sales success.

Higher educational advancement (as assessed quantitatively) was positively related to the mean but not the maximum sales volume rank. School achievement (as assessed qualitatively) was somewhat negatively correlated with mean sales volume rank.

School activities, vocational decisiveness, and professionally successful parents were found to be unrelated to sales success.

What the Research Suggests

Based upon the preceding review of prior research, several important conclusions can be drawn.

First, mental ability appears to be positively related to success in consumer sales. In general, the findings suggest that the greater the level of intelligence salespeople have, the more successful they are likely to be in their jobs. This tends to be true for general and social intelligence as well as for arithmetic ability. It should be noted, however, that intelligence may not always be positively related to success. Consumer salespeople in "high" grades of selling with higher levels of intelligence tend to be more successful; salespeople with lower levels of intelligence appear to be more successful in "low" grades of selling. The results thus suggest that managers should seek to hire relatively intelligent sales personnel as long as the sales position is not a "low" grade job. Sales personnel in "low" grade sales jobs should generally not exhibit extremely high levels of intelligence, since such people are likely to be lower performers. Managers should administer intelligence tests to prospective salespeople to ascertain the candidates' levels of intelligence. A variety of intelligence tests are available for administration (e.g., OTIS, WAIS), a few of which are cited in the appendix.

Second, results of studies measuring sociability generally suggest that salespeople who are externally oriented will be more successful than their internally oriented counterparts. In other words, salespersons who are empathic, extroverted, and genuinely like people tend to be more successful in consumer sales. Thus, sales managers should seek to hire sales personnel who exhibit an external, people-oriented perspective. This perspective may be detected by a personal interview with the candidate, by comments on the application where nonwork activities are noted, or by the administration of personality tests (see the appendix for examples of personality tests).

Third, measures of forcefulness—such as self assurance, self confidence, aggressiveness, dominance, ego drive, and aspiration (career) level—do not appear to be consistent predictors of success in consumer product sales. Although somewhat contradictory, most evidence suggests that confident, aggressive salespeople with high ego drives demonstrate higher levels of performance than their counterparts who exhibit low levels of these three characteristics. Thus, managers should consider recruiting individuals who are aggressive "go-getters" and who are confident of success. Personal interviews and personality tests may be useful for identifying these characteristics in a job candidate.

Only one study examined experience/background factors as predictors of success in consumer sales. That investigation showed that the extent of a person's family and financial responsibility was positively related to sales success. A narrow and legally questionable interpretation of this result suggests that managers may wish to hire individuals with dependents. Perhaps having dependents encourages a salesperson to seek a high level of performance. After all, higher performance should equate with more job rewards, which should mean more security for the salesperson's family. A broader interpretation is that recruits are more likely to be successful if they have already evidenced the willingness to accept and successfully discharge a variety of sales or nonsales responsibilities. This latter implication is clearly consistent with the current practice of searching for proven winners—almost regardless of their arena of success.

Summary

In this chapter we have examined research that has explored which physical characteristics, mental abilities, personality characteristics, and experience/ background factors of sales personnel are related to success in consumer product and service sales. Findings from thirteen studies suggest that salespeople with higher levels of intelligence are more successful than those with lower levels of intelligence. The opposite tends to be true, however, if a salesperson is in a "low" grade sales position. Also, salespersons who are empathic, extroverted, and like people tend to be more successful. Furthermore, it appears that confident, aggressive individuals with high ego drives are likely to be successful in consumer selling.

3
Industrial Product and Service Sales

T his chapter examines findings and conclusions of previous research that sought to identify variables that predict success in selling industrial products and services (see appendix, table A–2). Industrial sales personnel sell products or services intended for use in business, and sales are generally to resellers or end-users. The studies reviewed here employed samples of salespeople who marketed such products or services as office systems, agricultural supplies, building materials, steel strapping, and utilities. Nine studies were reviewed that focused on predictors of success in industrial sales.

What the Research Found

Physical Characteristics

Two studies explored the relationships between two physical characteristics (age and height) and success in industrial selling. Kirchner, McElwain, and Dunnette (1960) discovered that age was positively correlated with success in the 30- to 45-year-old age bracket, but unrelated in the less than 30- or greater than 45-year-old age bracket. Lamont and Lundstrom (1977) found that neither weight nor age was associated with sales success. They did find, however, that height was positively related to new business conversion and incentive earnings.

Mental Abilities

Results from previous empirical work are inconsistent concerning the relationships between mental abilities and success in industrial selling. For example, Bagozzi (1978, 1980a) determined that verbal intelligence was negatively correlated with sales success, but Perreault, French, and Harris (1977) discovered that a vocabulary measure (an assessment of intelligence) was unrelated to sales success. Perreault, French, and Harris (1977), however, ascertained that higher levels of mental ability and social intelligence were associated with better performance. Weitz (1978) found that "strategy formulation ability" (a type of mental ability) was positively related to sales success.

Personality Characteristics

Several studies have investigated relationships between sales success and personality characteristics of industrial sales personnel.

Sociability. A variety of sociability factors have been examined in prior research. Social recognition, desire for esteem, and empathy were found to be unrelated to success in industrial sales (Lamont and Lundstrom 1977). However, extroversion was determined to be positively associated with success (Howells 1968; Perreault, French, and Harris 1977), as were a sense of humor (Perreault, French, and Harris 1977) and complexity (Scheibelhut and Albaum 1973). Scheibelhut and Albaum (1973) discovered that inclusion, majority identification, social interest, and self centrality were not associated with sales success.

Forcefulness. Few variables assessing forcefulness have been examined in industrial sales studies. Dunnette and Kirchner (1960) found dominance to be positively related to sales success, but Lamont and Lundstrom (1977) and Perreault, French, and Harris (1977) found it unrelated. Ego strength has been shown to be unrelated to sales volume but negatively associated with managerial rating of performance (Lamont and Lundstrom 1977). Ego involvement, however, was positively correlated with success, as were vigor (Perreault, French, and Harris 1977), endurance (Lamont and Lundstrom 1977; Perreault, French, and Harris 1977; Howells 1968), and self esteem (Scheibelhut and Albaum 1973).

Experience/Background

The two studies that explored the association between experience/background factors and success in industrial selling examined only a limited number of variables. Lamont and Lundstrom (1977) determined that formal education, number of outside activities, and membership in professional and civic organizations were generally unrelated to sales success. Perreault, French, and Harris (1977) found that neither business skills nor sales aptitude was correlated with success in industrial selling.

What the Research Suggests

The results of the nine investigations do not suggest any general relationships between industrial sales success and specific physical characteristics, mental abilities, personality characteristics, and experience/background. However, there are certain relevant conclusions.

Apparently physical characteristics are not materially related to sales success. Height was positively related to two measures of sales performance, but only in one study. Age had only a very limited relationship with success. Thus, the research to date suggests that managers should not use physical characteristics of candidates as predictors of sales success.

Research results focusing on mental abilities indicate that some measures of intelligence (e.g., verbal intelligence) were not consistently correlated with sales success. Other intelligence measures (e.g., social intelligence), however, may be related to sales success. The research to date is too meager to offer industrial sales managers a clear indication of the relationship between mental abilities of candidates and their potential job success.

Few studies have employed similar variables when examining the association between sociability (personality characteristics) and sales success. There appears to be a positive relationship between sociability measures and sales success, but the results are inconsistent. Thus, managers should not look for specific sociability characteristics when seeking to identify personality factors in industrial sales success.

Although forcefulness was generally positively related to sales success, forcefulness was not a consistent predictor of sales success and, therefore, should be employed cautiously as a guide to selecting qualified industrial sales personnel. Two variables, dominance and endurance, were examined in more than one study. Endurance was positively associated with success in both studies, but dominance was related to success in one study but not the other. Separately, vigor, self esteem, and ego involvement were also positively associated with success.

Experience/background factors do not appear to be associated with industrial salesperson success. Thus, such factors do not offer managers clues concerning correct hiring decisions.

The lack of a clear multistudy conclusion about specific variables suggests that industrial selling requires a balanced combination of characteristics rather than one or two dominant characteristics. Additional research may bear this out.

Summary

In this chapter we discussed empirical work examining predictors of success in selling industrial products and services. Research results from nine investigations indicate that—at least for the variables studied—physical characteristics, mental abilities, personality characteristics, and experience/background factors are poor predictors of sales success. The findings from these studies either identified little relationship between sales success and potential predictors or were inconsistent. A potential explanation for this situation may be that the industrial sales job requires a combination of salesperson characteristics that is well-balanced, rather than consisting of one or a few characteristics.

4
Life Insurance Sales

C hapter 4 reviews studies that explored variables potentially predicting success in life insurance sales, and examines the studies'
implications (see appendix, table A–3). The process of selling life
insurance involves several key steps. These steps are prospecting, the pre-
approach, the approach, fact-finding, designing the solution, presenting the
solution, the close, sales follow-through, policy delivery, and commitment to
service (*Steps into Sales* 1981). In addition, life insurance has been called a
"regularly unsought good"—that is, a product that a consumer will probably
eventually buy but is not motivated to buy (McCarthy 1981). Consequently,
aggressive and diligent selling efforts generally may be needed to consummate
this kind of sale. The research results discussed in this chapter are based upon
a review of six published studies.

What the Research Found

Physical Characteristics

Prior research exploring relationships between physical characteristics and
success in insurance selling has not been very revealing. Age has been examined in two studies and found to be unrelated to sales success (Merenda and
Clarke 1959; Tanofsky, Shepps, and O'Neill 1969).

Evans (1963) investigated success in selling life insurance by focusing on
the agent-customer dyad. Using age, income, height, religion, political affiliation, and smoking habits as predictor variables, he found that agents were
more likely to make a sale when they were more similar to their prospects in
terms of these characteristics than when they were less similar. Evans con-
cluded that clients who bought life insurance were more likely than those not
buying to:

Consider the agent a friend;

Believe the agent liked them;

Enjoy their conversations with the agent;

Think that the agent enjoyed his or her job.

The first three conclusions appear to describe an empathic relationship between agent and client. The fourth may connote an agent who is satisfied with his or her job, personally involved, and self confident. Notwithstanding Evans's findings, Weitz (1979) raises serious doubts about the validity of the salesperson-customer similarity hypothesis. Moreover, Churchill, Collins, and Strang (1975), using a retail sales site, found no support for Evans's results.

Mental Abilities

No studies employing samples of life insurance agents examined relationships between mental abilities and sales success.

Personality Characteristics

Only two studies were identified that explored personality characteristics of successful life insurance agents.

Sociability. Merenda and Clarke (1959) discovered that sociability was positively correlated with sales success and social adaptability was negatively related. Empathy has been shown to be positively associated with sales success (Greenberg and Mayer 1964).

Forcefulness. Aggressiveness has been found to be positively correlated with sales success and emotional control negatively related (Merenda and Clarke 1959). Greenberg and Mayer (1964) determined that ego strength was positively associated with sales success.

Experience/Background

Although five investigations examined relationships between experience/background variables and success in life insurance sales, few common variables have been shared by the studies. Education has been shown to be both positively related (Merenda and Clarke 1959) and unrelated (Tanofsky, Shepps, and O'Neill 1969) to sales success. Number of dependents was positively associated with success (Brown 1978; Merenda and Clarke 1959; Tanofsky, Shepps, and O'Neill 1969). Number of organizational memberships and offices held in organizations (Brown 1978; Merenda and Clarke 1959), marital status (Merenda and Clarke 1959; Tanofsky, Shepps, and

O'Neill 1969), and sales experience (Merenda and Clarke 1959; Tanofsky, Shepps, and O'Neill 1969) have been found to be unrelated to sales success. Other experience/background factors, examined in only one study, however, have been found to have the following relationships with sales success:

Number of sales courses and wife's employment status: no relationship (Merenda and Clarke 1959);

Product knowledge and sales training: positive relationship (Baier and Dugan 1957);

Time spent with most recent employer: positive relationship (Brown 1978).

The amount of life insurance owned by the agent (Baier and Dugan 1957; Brown 1978; Merenda and Clarke 1959) has been positively correlated with sales success. Other financial characteristics have been shown to be positively related to success in life insurance sales (but not in more than one study). These financial variables are monthly living expenses (Merenda and Clarke 1959), prior income (Tanofsky, Shepps, and O'Neill 1969), minimum current living expenses (Brown 1978), and net worth (Brown 1978). In addition, military status, education expenses earned, years at present residence, unearned income, debts, recreational activities, and number of friends were found not to be associated with sales success (Merenda and Clarke 1959).

What the Research Suggests

Most research that examined predictors of success in life insurance selling explored primarily physical characteristics and experience/background factors. Overall, the results of these investigations do not provide clear guidance concerning the recruitment and selection of life insurance agents. This situation exists for three reasons: (1) few common variables have been shared by the studies: (2) research results for the same variable are often inconsistent; and (3) most studies have found no relationship between sales success and the variables under study. Despite this dilemma, some tentative conclusions may be drawn.

First, agents who exhibit empathy appear to be more successful than those who do not. Thus, insurance sales managers may wish to hire agents who are empathic. Empathy may be detected through a personal interview with the candidate, through a mock sales presentation given by the candidate, or through the administration of relevant personality tests.

Second, agents who are aggressive and autonomous appear to be more successful than those lacking these qualities. Thus, candidates possessing these characteristics should be considered potentially good agents. However, the aggressiveness must not be so strong that it interferes with the empathetic relationship. To assess candidates' levels of aggressiveness and independence, personality tests could be given.

Finally, certain background and experiential variables are positively associated with sales. However, the vast majority of the insurance agents studied were at least somewhat successful in selling insurance. Consequently, it is not at all clear whether these variables (e.g., amount of insurance owned) lead to, or are caused by, sales success.

Summary

In this chapter we explored potential relationships between success in selling life insurance and physical characteristics, mental abilities, personality characteristics, and experience/background factors. Most prior research has focused on physical characteristics and experience/background factors and their association with sales success. Although only tentative, the results of prior investigations indicate that the more successful life insurance agent will exhibit empathy and manifest a modicum of aggressiveness and independence.

5
Retail Sales

T his chapter reviews studies that have sought to identify predictors of success in retail sales and examines the studies' implications (see appendix, table A–4). Traditionally, the retail salesperson has been viewed as an "order filler," as someone who performs mundane tasks and "rings up" the sale. In today's intensely competitive environment, however, some retail sales personnel play a major role in the success of a retail outlet. In fact, prior research has found that retail salespeople are an important element in a retailer's marketing-service mix (Berry 1969; Burstiner 1975–1976; Claxton and Ritchie 1979; Hansen and Deutscher 1977–1978; Jolson and Spath 1973). Thus, hiring qualified retail sales personnel should be a goal of any retailer. Eight studies were examined that investigated predictors of success in retail sales.

What the Research Found

Physical Characteristics

Several physical characteristics were examined in terms of their relationships with sales success. The results, however, are ambiguous. Age was determined to be both positively related (Mosel 1952; Weaver 1969) and unrelated (Cotham 1969; French 1960) to success in retail selling. Mosel (1952) found that weight, height, and domicile were unrelated to sales success.

Using a retail setting, Churchill, Collins, and Strang (1975) tested Evans's (1963) similarity hypothesis, which states that the more a salesperson is similar to the prospect, the more likely a sale will be made. Similarity was compared using age, height, sex, race, nationality, religion, political affiliation, and education. Their research did not support the similarity hypothesis.

Mental Abilities

Only one study was found that employed a sample of retail sales personnel when examining relationships between mental abilities and sales success.

Ghiselli (1973) discovered that several measures of mental ability (e.g., intelligence and motor ability) were unrelated to sales success.

Personality Characteristics

Four studies examined personality characteristics of retail salespersons.

Sociability. French (1960) indicated that favorable coworker relations were inversely related to sales success. Spivey, Munson, and Locander (1979) discovered that an outgoing personality was positively associated and an external orientation inversely related to sales success. Finally, higher social status was found to be positively related to sales success (French 1960).

Forcefulness. No direct measures of forcefulness (such as dominance, self esteem, or self confidence) were employed in the retail sales studies. However, some variables that approximate forcefulness measures have been used in retail sales settings. Cotham (1968) found that vigor was positively related but feelings of personal worth unrelated to sales success. Weaver (1969) discovered that a salesperson's perceived power was positively associated with sales success.

Experience/Background

Few common experience/background variables were examined by the studies. Where multiple investigations explored a particular experience/background variable, the findings tended to be inconsistent. For example, education was found to be positively related (Mosel 1952; Weaver 1969) and unrelated (Cotham 1969; French 1960) to sales success. Experience has been shown to be both positively correlated (Mosel 1952) and unrelated (Cotham 1969; French 1960) to sales success, as has number of dependents (Mosel 1952; Spivey, Munson, and Locander 1979). Also, Cotham (1969) ascertained that number of club memberships was not correlated and that having a working wife was negatively correlated with sales success. Married salespeople have been found to be more successful than unmarried ones (Mosel 1952; Weaver 1969). Number of hours worked has been shown to be positively related to sales success (Spivey, Munson, and Locander 1979), but time lost on the job negatively related (Mosel 1952).

What the Research Suggests

Research to date that has examined predictors of success in retail selling has not yielded a clear answer to the question, Whom should the retail sales manager hire? Few common variables have been examined by the studies, and where multiple studies have explored a particular variable, results tend to be inconsistent. However, research results lead to some conclusions.

First, no physical characteristic studied appears to be strongly associated with sales success. Thus, the evaluation of physical characteristics in the recruiting process does not seem to be a viable approach to hiring retail salespeople.

Second, since mental abilities have not been extensively examined to date, no conclusion can be drawn about judging on the basis of mental abilities during the hiring process.

Third, although not thoroughly examined, sociability and forcefulness do not appear to be important predictors of sales success in retail selling. Tentatively, however, it seems that individuals exhibiting vigor and having a high degree of perceived power are more successful in retail sales than those without these characteristics. Thus, retail sales managers may wish to hire personnel who demonstrate these two qualities. Evidence of vigor and perceived power could be obtained by administering appropriate personality tests to candidates. However, more research is needed to clarify the personality characteristics–sales success linkages in retail selling.

In general, because of the inconsistency in results for experience/background variables, additional research is needed to identify relevant (if any) experience/background variables that may predict sales success in retail selling.

Summary

This chapter reviewed research from eight studies that explored predictors of success in retail sales. A variety of physical characteristics, mental abilities, personality characteristics, and experience/background factors have been examined in terms of relationships with sales success. The results of these investigations generally provide no clear guidelines to what kind of salesperson a retail sales manager should hire. Much additional empirical work is needed to identify predictors of success in retail sales.

Part II
Managing Sales Personnel

I n part I of this book we examined potential characteristics or factors
that may predict sales success and thus may be useful in the recruitment
and selection process. Once salespeople have been hired, trained, and
assigned to a territory, managing the sales force for productive results
becomes the manager's primary responsibility.

Porter and Lawler (1968) created a model of the factors that influence
employee performance. Their model identified four factors: motivation, role
clarity and acceptance, employee abilities and traits, and opportunity to perform. Assuming that the recruiting and selection process has been effective in
hiring people with the correct abilities and traits, sales managers must be concerned with salesperson motivation, role perceptions, job satisfaction, and
job performance. Figure II–1 illustrates how job satisfaction and performance may be either directly affected by personal factors, structural factors,
and managerial actions, or indirectly affected by these factors through the
linking stages of motivation and role perceptions. Because the terms dis-
played in figure II–1 will be used throughout part II, they are defined below:

Personal factors are characteristics that describe the individual salesperson. Examples of these are age, sex, income level, education, training,
marital status, self esteem, and vocational maturity.

Structural factors are intra- or extra-organizational variables and include
job design, organizational design, span of control, company policies and
procedures, level of competition, and economic conditions.

Managerial actions represent the behaviors exhibited by managers when
supervising their subordinates. Examples include type of power/influ-
ence, degree of closeness of supervision, willingness to allow subordinates to participate in decision making, and degree of subordinate's job
autonomy.

Motivation represents an employee's desire to expend effort on the job
or on particular aspects of the job.

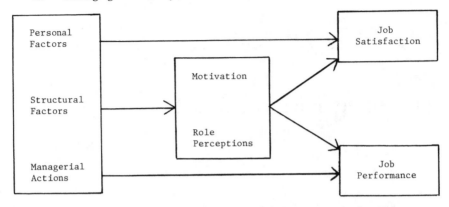

Figure II–1. Model of Salesperson Satisfaction and Performance

Role perceptions are the role conflict and ambiguity experienced by an individual. Role conflict occurs when an individual receives incompatible job demands or expectations from two or more parties that cannot be satisfied simultaneously (e.g., the customer demands a price discount but the company does not permit salespeople to sell below list price). Role ambiguity occurs when an individual has inadequate knowledge or information with which to perform the job.

Job satisfaction refers to the affective reactions (feelings) an employee has toward his or her work situation.

Job performance indicates how well an employee executes his or her job tasks, responsibilities, and assignments. This may be a quantitative or qualitative assessment in relation to some standard.

The three chapters in part II review the prior research that has examined the nature of the relationships between personal factors, structural factors, and managerial actions and the salesperson. More specifically, they examine the relationships between these three variables and:

Motivation and role perceptions (chapter 6)

Job satisfaction (chapter 7)

Job performance (chapter 8)

6
Motivation and Role Perceptions

T his chapter looks at three elements—personal factors, structural factors, and managerial actions—that are associated with salespeople's motivation and role perceptions. Prior to this discussion, a brief theoretical view of motivation and role perceptions is presented to provide the reader with an understanding of the complexities of salesperson motivation and role perceptions.

Motivation

As noted earlier, motivation is an employee's desire to expend effort on the job. Motivation has been extensively researched by both psychologists and organizational behaviorists. Steers (1981, p. 42) provides a generally accepted definition of motivation "as that which energizes, directs, and sustains human behavior." He goes on to identify three important aspects of motivation.

> First, motivation represents an energetic force which *drives* people to behave in particular ways. Second, this drive is directed *toward* something. In other words, motivation has a strong goal orientation. Third, the idea of motivation is best understood within a *systems* perspective. That is, to understand human motivation, it is necessary to examine the forces within individuals and their environments that provide them with feedback and reinforce their intensity and direction.

Historically, in sales management "money as motivator" has been the dominant theory of motivation. Thus, for years researchers paid particular attention to developing the best compensation plan that simultaneously motivated salespeople and achieved organizational objectives. The alternative compensation plans and the situations for which they are appropriate have been presented in the literature (e.g., Day and Bennett 1962; Steinbrink 1978; Tosdal 1953). Other writers have opted for a modeling approach to designing an "optimal" compensation plan (Darmon 1974, 1979; Farley 1964). Winer (1973), however, demonstrated that while "optimal" compensation plans may be theoretically appealing, they are administratively difficult to implement.

The research evidence has demonstrated that adequate, timely compensation is a necessary but insufficient motivator of sales personnel. In fact, research results indicate that a compensation plan may have widely different effects, depending upon the salesperson being affected by it (Darmon 1974). Moreover, compensation may be more motivating for some kinds of salespeople than for others (Churchill, Ford, and Walker 1979).

A more recent motivational theory that has received a great deal of research in sales management is Vroom's expectancy theory (Vroom 1964). This theory views people as being intelligent, rational individuals who make conscious decisions about their present and future behavior. In this theory, people are not seen as inherently motivated or unmotivated. Rather, people's motivational levels are viewed as a function of their work environment: as long as that work environment is consistent with their goals and needs, they are motivated.

Walker, Churchill, and Ford (1977) adapted the basic Vroom model to the sales management environment. Their adaptation is:

$$M_i = \sum_{j=1}^{n} E_{ij} \times \left(\sum_{k=1}^{m} I_{jk} \times V_k \right)$$

M_i = motivation: ". . . a salesman's motivation to expend effort on any task (i)."

E_{ij} = expectancy: ". . . the salesman's estimate of the probability that expending a given amount of effort on task (i) will lead to an improved level of performance on some performance dimension (j)."

I_{jk} = instrumentality: ". . . the salesman's estimate of the probability that achieving an improved level of performance on performance dimension (j) will lead to increased attainment of a particular reward (k) or outcome."

V_k = valence for rewards: ". . . the salesman's perceptions of the desirability of receiving increased amounts of each of a variety of rewards he might attain as a result of improved performance."

According to expectancy theory, salespeople's motivation (not performance) is a result of their effort-performance expectations multiplied by their performance-outcome expectancies multiplied by the reward valences for those outcomes.

For example, assume that a salesperson strongly believes (9 on a scale from 1 to 10, or .9) that an increased number of calls per week (effort) will generate higher sales. This person would have a high effort-performance expectancy. If this same person also believes (.8) that such a sales increase will cause him or her to win a sales contest, we can say that he or she has a high performance-outcome expectancy. Moreover, if winning this contest is extremely important (+ .9 on a − 1.0 to + 1.0 scale), then we can conclude that this salesperson has a relatively high motivational force (.9 × .8 × .9 = .65). If, however, all other things are equal, but the contest prize has little value for a salesperson (.2), then the motivational force would be much lower (.9 × .8 × .2 = .14). Thus, all three components must be high for high motivational levels to exist. (Adapted from Steers 1981.)

Campbell and Pritchard (1976) reviewed thirty-five studies that tested the Vroom Expectancy-Instrumentality-Valence (VIE) Theory in an organizational setting. In general, they found from a statistical perspective that each of the three components/outcomes (expectancy, instrumentality, and valence) of the Vroom model was moderately and independently related to effort and performance. Performance and each of the three outcomes were found to be particularly strongly related. However:

> There seem to be less than satisfactory correlations (usually less than .30) between the full Vroom model and independent measures of expended effort. A multiplicative model seemed to be better than an additive one.

> Most of the variance in expended effort is accounted for by either expectancy or instrumentality. Multiplication by valence (reward) usually did not improve the explanatory power of the model.

> Some research results indicate that performance-outcome relationships that are associated with internally mediated outcomes are more important than those attached to externally mediated outcomes. This means that an individual's personal goals are more important or stimulating than someone else's. If a manager can link organizational goals to a subordinate's goals, then motivation is enhanced.

These less than ringing endorsements from the empirical testing of the model spawned a plethora of reviews, reexaminations, and reformulations (e.g., Connolly 1976; Dillard 1981; Einhorn 1971; Graen 1969; Payne 1976; Porter and Lawler 1968; Schmidt 1973; Simon 1956; Schwab, Gottlieb, and Heneman 1979). The details of these revisions are beyond the scope of this review and do not substantially alter the Vroom concept and model as tested by researchers in organizational behavior (Matsui et al. 1977) and sales management (e.g., Oliver 1974; Teas 1980, 1981b).

Role Perceptions

Numerous definitions of the word *role* exist. A common theme of most definitions focuses on role in relation to a *position*. Position typically is used to designate the niche or status of a group of individuals within a social structure. A role, then, is the pattern of behavior of a person occupying a position (or niche) and is the linkage between an individual and the social structure. In terms of sales management, three role-related constructs deserve special attention here. They are role set, role conflict, and role ambiguity.

Role Set

A role set consists of the individuals (role partners) with whom the role occupant (e.g., a salesperson) has role relationships. A salesperson's role set may include primarily company management, fellow salespeople, other company employees, customers, and family members. Thus, sales personnel have a large number of role partners with whom they interact. Salespeople also have a number of different roles to play, as can be seen in figure 6–1. A salesperson has a role as an employee, customer consultant, family member, friend, and community member. With their multiple roles and role partners, salespeople are likely to experience role conflict.

Role Conflict

Role conflict occurs when different role partners have contradictory expectations for their shared role partner (Parsons 1951). For example, a customer may demand that the salesperson provide terms that are 2–10, net 30, but the salesperson's management offers only net 30 terms. The salesperson cannot keep both role partners (the customer and management) satisfied, and thus role conflict is experienced.

Contrary expectations of a role partner produce conflict between role relationships in the role set. This situation induces conflict in the individual confronting the conflicting expectations and disturbs the entire role set. The conflict engenders disturbance, which might be alleviated through avoidance, compromise, conformity, or severance of the relationship.

Role Ambiguity

In theory, every organizational position should have clearly defined tasks and responsibilities. Role ambiguity arises when these tasks are ill defined or not defined at all (Levinson 1975). The occupant of this ill-defined position typically experiences stress because of uncertainty or lack of clarity. The stress evokes certain coping mechanisms designed to reduce stress, such as attempts at clarification or reality distortion. Individuals experiencing role ambiguity usually are dissatisfied in their role and have higher anxiety levels

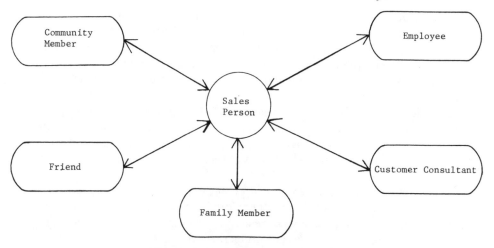

Figure 6–1. A Salesperson's Roles

and lower levels of performance (Kahn et al. 1964; Rizzo, House, and Lirtz-man 1970). For detailed discussions about a salesperson's roles, see, for example, Belasco (1966), Hise (1970), and Walker, Churchill, and Ford (1972).

Research on Salesperson Motivation

We have noted that three elements—personal factors, structural factors, and managerial actions—may be associated with salesperson motivation (see appendix, table A–5). Several studies have examined motivation as related to these factors. When exploring motivation, researchers either have directly measured motivation or assessed it using some form of Vroom model. Previous studies that have explored the relationship between each of the elements and salesperson motivation are now presented.

Personal Factors and Motivation

Seven studies examined the association between personal factors and sales-person motivation. Few variables were tested in more than one investigation.

Direct Assessment of Motivation. Two studies assessed motivation directly. Doyle and Shapiro (1980) found that an industrial salesperson's need for achievement was positively related to motivation (defined as the number of hours spent per week in selling activities). Dubinsky and Skinner (1984b) showed that part-time and full-time retail salespeople have comparable levels of work motivation.

Vroom Model of Motivation. Several investigators have examined personal factors and their relationships to motivation using a Vroom model of motivation. Teas (1981b) found that specific self esteem was positively related but global self esteem, job experience, and internal orientation were unrelated to industrial salespeople's expectancies. He also discovered that internal orientation was positively related to industrial salespeople's global instrumentalities. Using a retail sales sample, Teas (1982) discovered that internal orientation was positively associated with global instrumentality as well as with self fulfillment, company relationships, growth, and direct performance recognition instrumentality. The results of these two studies are portrayed in figure 6–2.

Two investigations focused on salespeople's valences for various rewards. Churchill, Ford, and Walker (1979) explored whether certain personal factors of industrial salespeople were related to their valences for lower-order rewards (pay, security) and higher-order rewards (recognition, promotion, liking and respect, sense of accomplishment, and personal growth). They found that job tenure, age, and family size (but not marital status or education) were generally positively related to these reward valences. Ingram and Bellenger (1983) also used an industrial sales sample and the same seven reward valences as Churchill, Ford, and Walker (1979). They, however, found that age, job tenure, family size, education, income level, vocational maturity, and specific self esteem were generally unrelated to those reward valences.

Structural Factors and Motivation

A number of studies have examined structural factors and their relationships to salesperson motivation. Although some investigations employed similar structural factors, their assessments of motivation usually differed (see figure 6–3).

Direct Assessment of Motivation. Five studies assessed motivation directly. Futrell (1979) found that nine job design factors (e.g., clarity of results, clarity of goal importance, control, and influence) were unrelated to pharmaceutical salespeople's intrinsic motivation. Doyle and Shapiro (1980) discovered that task clarity was positively related to industrial salespeople's motivation and that an incentive pay compensation plan was more motivating than a salary compensation plan. Tyagi (1982) examined the relationship between five structural factors and insurance salespeople's extrinsic and intrinsic motivation. He found that intrinsic motivation was unrelated to job challenge and variety, positively related to job importance and organizational identification, and inversely associated with task conflict and role overload. Extrinsic motivation was positively related to job importance and organiza-

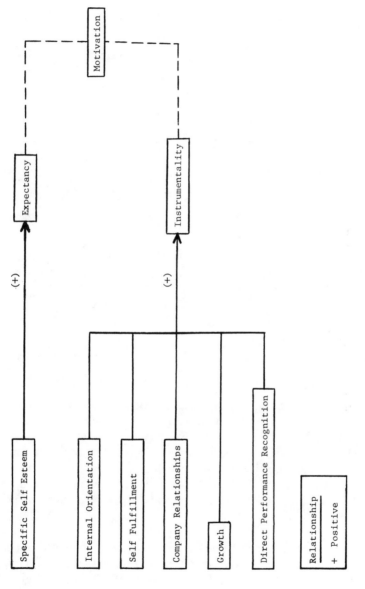

Figure 6–2. Personal Factors and Vroom Motivation Model

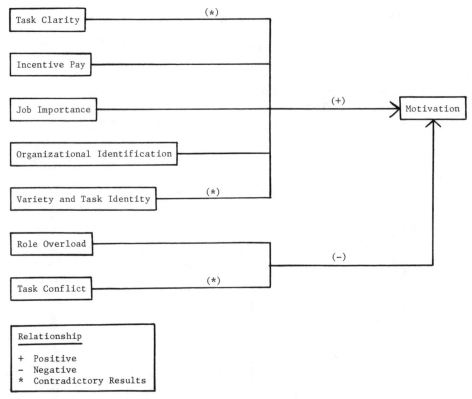

Figure 6–3. Structural Factors and Direct Motivation Assessment

tional identification, negatively related to task conflict, and unrelated to the other two structural factors. Using a retail sales sample, Dubinsky and Skinner (1984a) found that work motivation was positively associated with variety and task identity, negatively related to role ambiguity, and not associated with autonomy, job-provided feedback, or role conflict. Becherer, Morgan, and Richard (1982) showed that two characteristics relating to the quality of the job (meaningfulness and responsibility) were positively related to internal work motivation.

Vroom Model of Motivation. Several studies have employed a Vroom model to assess the relationships between structural factors and salesperson motivation (see figure 6–4). Part of the work of Teas (1981b) and Tyagi (1982) focused on salespeople's expectancy and instrumentality estimates. Teas (1981b) found that industrial salespeople's expectancy estimates were positively associated with task variety, completeness, task complexity; inversely

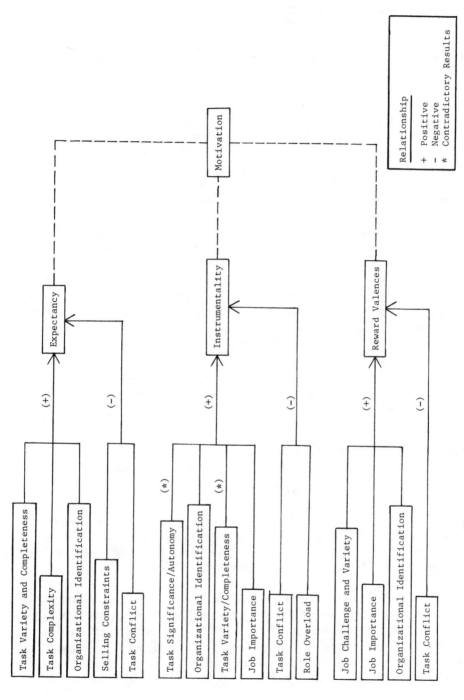

Figure 6–4. Structural Factors and Vroom Motivation Model

related to perceived selling constraints; and unrelated to job significance/ autonomy. He also determined that global instrumentality was positively associated with task significance/autonomy and task variety/completeness, and unrelated to task complexity and job-provided feedback. Tyagi (1982) ascertained that organizational identification was positively associated, and task conflict negatively related, to expectancy estimates. Moreover, he found that intrinsic instrumentality estimates were positively associated with job importance and organizational identification, and inversely related to task conflict and role overload. He also discovered that extrinsic instrumentality estimates were positively associated with job importance. Teas (1982) discovered that job-provided feedback, task variety, task significance, and task autonomy were generally unrelated to the following instrumentalities of retail salespeople: self fulfillment, company relationships, growth, and direct performance recognition.

Three investigations explored the relationships between structural factors and salespeople's reward valences. Tyagi (1980) determined that insurance salespeople's intrinsic and extrinsic valences were positively related to job challenge and variety and job importance, but not associated with organizational identification or job autonomy. Tyagi (1982) also ascertained that intrinsic valences were positively related to organizational identification and that extrinsic valences were inversely associated with task conflict. Ingram and Bellenger (1983) investigated whether the types of compensation plan, promotion opportunity rate, recognition rate, or earnings opportunity rate were related to industrial salespeople's valence for seven rewards. Study results generally showed no relationships between the four structural factors and seven reward valences.

Managerial Actions and Motivation

Few studies have explored the relationships between managerial actions and salesperson motivation (see figure 6–5).

Direct Assessment of Motivation. Only one investigation assessed motivation directly. Tyagi (1982) found that leadership consideration and management concern and awareness were positively associated with intrinsic motivation but unrelated to extrinsic motivation.

Vroom Model of Motivation. Two researchers employed a Vroom model to assess motivation. Teas (1981b) found that industrial salespeople's expectancy estimates were positively related to salesperson participation in decision making, but unrelated to manager-provided feedback, consideration, and initiation of structure. He also ascertained that participation and consideration were positively related, but initiation of structure unrelated, to global

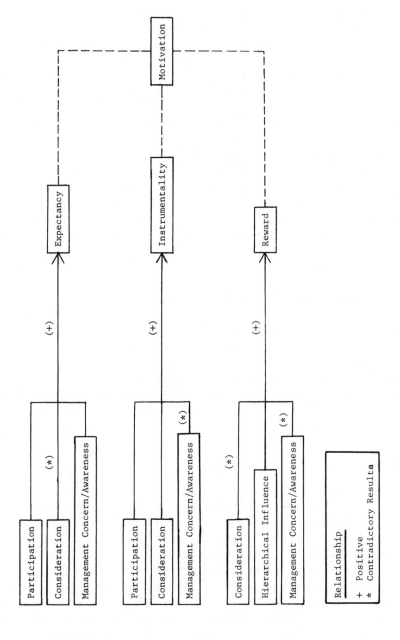

Figure 6–5. Managerial Actions and Vroom Motivation Model

instrumentality. Tyagi (1982) discerned that an insurance salesperson's expectancy estimates were positively associated with consideration and management concern and awareness. He also discovered that consideration was positively related to intrinsic and extrinsic instrumentality, and that management concern and awareness were positively related to intrinsic instrumentality and unrelated to extrinsic instrumentality. In another study Teas (1982) used four different measures of instrumentalities (self fulfillment, company relationships, growth, direct performance recognition). He determined that consideration was positively associated with two of the measures and that initiation of structure and manager-provided feedback were positively related to only one. (See table A–5 for specifics on the instrumentalities).

One investigator explored relationships between managerial actions and salesperson reward valences. Tyagi (1980) determined that valences for intrinsic rewards were positively related to a leader's hierarchical influence but unrelated to consideration. The opposite situation prevailed, however, for extrinsic rewards. Tyagi (1982) also ascertained that management concern and awareness were positively related to salespeople's intrinsic, but not extrinsic, reward valences.

Research on Salesperson Role Perceptions

The role perceptions of sales personnel have been a popular topic for researchers in the field of sales management, particularly within the past ten years (see appendix, table A–6). Eleven studies were reviewed that focused on the relationships between the three elements—personal factors, structural factors, and managerial actions—*and* role conflict and/or ambiguity. Most of the investigations focused on the variables that may impact role ambiguity, but a few studies explored the variables that may affect role conflict.

Personal Factors and Role Perceptions

Job tenure (time in position) has been found to be positively related (Dubinsky and Borys 1981), negatively related (Walker, Churchill, and Ford 1975), and unrelated (Teas 1983) to salespeople's role conflict. In addition, comparisons of part-time and full-time retail salespeople found similar levels of role conflict (Dubinsky and Skinner 1984b) as did comparisons of retail salesmen and saleswomen (Dubinsky and Mattson 1980).

Job tenure has been found to be negatively associated with role ambiguity (Dubinsky and Borys 1981; Walker, Churchill, and Ford 1975) and unrelated to it (Teas 1983). Bush and Busch (1981) determined that salesperson age was not associated with role clarity (low role ambiguity). Also, Dubinsky and Skinner (1984b) discovered that part- and full-time retail salespersons have comparable levels of role ambiguity. Salesmen have been found to have greater role clarity (lower role ambiguity) than saleswomen (Busch and Bush 1978) as well as similar levels of role ambiguity (Dubinsky and Mattson 1980).

Structural Factors and Role Perceptions

Three studies focused on relationships between structural factors and salespeople's role perceptions. Industrial salesperson role conflict and ambiguity have been found to be positively related to manager's span of control (Chonko 1982). The number of departments in the salesperson's firm that affects sales job activities as well as the innovativeness required of the job have been shown to be unrelated to role conflict and ambiguity (Walker, Churchill, and Ford 1975). Dubinsky and Skinner (1984a) found that retail salesperson role conflict was inversely related to autonomy and job-provided feedback and unrelated to variety and task identity. Furthermore, they showed that role ambiguity was inversely associated with autonomy and task identity but unrelated to variety and job-provided feedback.

Managerial Actions

Most of the research on variables affecting salespeople's role perceptions has focused on how the actions of the sales manager may affect salesperson role conflict and ambiguity (see figure 6–6). Industrial salesperson role conflict has been found to be unrelated to closeness of supervision, salesperson influence on determining performance standards, and frequency of contact with the manager (Walker, Churchill, and Ford 1975). Teas (1983), however, obtained different results. Role conflict was inversely related to consideration as well as to participation (which is similar to influence on determining standards), and positively associated with initiation of structure (which is similar to high levels of closeness of supervision and frequency of contact).

Walker, Churchill, and Ford (1975) also determined that salesperson role ambiguity is inversely associated with closeness of supervision and influence in determining standards, but unrelated to frequency of contact. Somewhat similarly, role ambiguity has been found to be inversely related to manager-provided feedback and participation (Teas, Wacker, and Hughes 1979; Teas 1983) and consideration, but unrelated to initiation of structure (Teas 1983).

Busch (1980) examined the power (influence) pharmaceutical sales managers have over their sales personnel. Using salespeople from three companies and measuring five sources of power (expert, referent, legitimate, reward, and coercive), he found that role clarity (the opposite of role ambiguity) was positively associated with expert, referent, and legitimate power in two of the three samples. Reward and coercive power appeared to have little impact on salesperson role clarity.

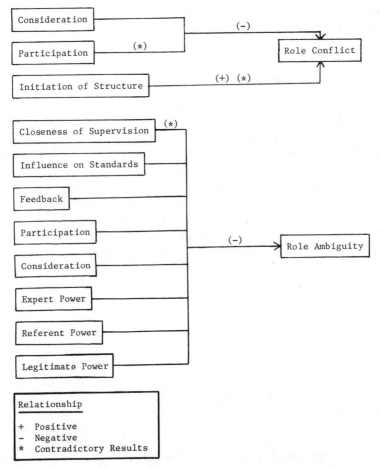

Figure 6–6. Managerial Actions and Role Conflict/Ambiguity

What the Research Suggests about Motivation

Researchers have employed two different approaches to assessing salesperson motivation: measuring motivation directly or measuring motivation with various components (expectancy, instrumentality, valence, and intrinsic or extrinsic motivation) of a Vroom model. The focus of the studies reviewed was to determine how to enhance salesperson motivation in terms of personal, structural, and managerial action factors.

Based upon the studies conducted to date, some personal factors appear to be indirectly related to salesperson motivation. Although some may con-

tend that certain kinds of salespeople may be more amenable to certain rewards (a component of motivation) than other kinds of salespeople, research
results are too scarce and inconsistent to support this contention. Thus,
research results do not support the direct use of personal factors to assist
managers in enhancing salesperson motivation.

Certain structural factors appear to be potentially useful for enhancing
motivation. Job importance tends to be a motivating influence, as are task
variety, task completeness, and job challenge. These results suggest that the
salesperson's job should be designed so that a multiplicity of tasks are performed. The tasks should not be mundane, however, but make a significant
contribution to the firm. Moreover, the job should afford sales personnel
with the opportunity to begin and complete an assignment in its entirety
(e.g., approach a prospect, make the sales presentation, close the sale, and
service the customer). Management should also seek to impart to salespeople
the significance of the job they perform so that they will realize they are an
integral part of the organization.

The manager, through his or her actions, may enhance salesperson motivation. Managers who exhibit concern and awareness as well as consideration (encouragement) for their sales personnel should have more motivated
salespeople than those who do not manifest these characteristics. Managers
should try to be supportive of their salespeople and to take a genuine interest
in their salespeople's job-related activities. Also, salesperson motivation tends
to be higher when they participate in making decisions that affect their jobs.
Consequently, sales managers should consider allowing their salespeople to
take an active role in determining performance standards, policies, and procedures that impact the salesperson's position.

Salesperson motivation apparently is reduced when salespeople receive
disparate expectations from role partners. More specifically, task conflict
and role overload were found to impair salesperson motivation. Thus, managers should attempt to design the work environment so that the salespeople
can manage effectively their on-the-job conflicts.

What the Research Suggests about Role Perceptions

Salesperson role perceptions have been frequently researched by researchers
in the field of sales management. The investigations have focused predom-
inantly on role ambiguity and potential causes of it, but some attention has
been given to the precursors of role conflict. Based upon the prior research
reviewed, several conclusions are forthcoming.

First, personal factors have received only minimal attention in the sales
management literature in terms of their relationships with role conflict and
ambiguity. The research that does exist is not illuminating. Thus, sales man-

agers cannot presently use personal factors to suggest which sales personnel will experience more or less role conflict and ambiguity.

Second, few structural factors have been investigated in terms of their relationships with role conflict and ambiguity. Tentatively, it appears that these two phenomena increase as the number of salespeople a manager supervises increases. Perhaps this occurs because managers have less time to assist their sales personnel as the number of salespeople they supervise grows, and thus their assistance in resolving salespersons' conflicts and clarifying their assignments may be reduced.

Third, results concerning the impact of managerial actions on salespeople's role conflict have been inconsistent, particularly with regard to closeness of supervision and participation. Consequently, it is unclear at this time how role conflict might be reduced by the sales manager.

Finally, the sales manager apparently can affect salespeople's level of role ambiguity. Closely supervising salespeople allows managers to clarify the salespeople's roles for them. Allowing salespeople to participate in relevant decision making and to influence standards helps them learn and understand the roles they perform. These activities should be employed by sales managers because they tend to reduce salespeople's role ambiguity without any dollar expenditures. Also, the use of expert, legitimate, and referent power by the sales manager may help clarify the salesperson's role.

Summary

In this chapter research studies were reviewed that examined linkages between motivation and role perceptions and personal factors, structural factors, and managerial actions. Salesperson motivation appears to be unrelated to personal factors, but it does seem to be enhanced when salespeople hold positions that involve performing a variety of significant tasks and that require performance of an entire assignment. Motivation is also higher when managers exhibit concern for their sales personnel, are supportive, allow salespeople to have input into decisions that affect their jobs, and help them reduce their job conflicts.

Personal factors apparently are unrelated to salesperson's role conflict and ambiguity, but span of control is positively associated with these two role perceptions. Although there may be little managers can do to reduce salespeople's role conflict, they can help decrease role ambiguity. This may be done by closely supervising sales personnel, allowing them participation in relevant decisions, and using noncoercive sources of power.

7
Job Satisfaction

J ob satisfaction, as noted earlier, is the affective reaction (feelings) an
employee has toward his or her work situation. In everyday terms, job
satisfaction would indicate how pleased employees are with such
aspects of their jobs as pay, benefits, coworkers, supervisors, company policies and procedures, the job itself, recognition, promotion opportunities, and
working conditions. Job satisfaction is an important concern of sales managers because it appears to be related to salesperson absenteeism, turnover,
and motivation (Walker, Churchill, and Ford 1979) and may be linked to
performance (Bagozzi 1980a; Futrell et al. 1983).

In this review of the findings from previous research concerning salesperson job satisfaction, the results will be discussed in the following order:
motivation, role perceptions, personal factors, structural factors, and managerial actions. It should be noted that, although researchers have measured
salesperson job satisfaction in different ways, all of the investigations reviewed were essentially tapping the same basic dimension of job satisfaction (see
appendix, table A–7).

Motivation and Job Satisfaction

Only one researcher examined the linkage between salesperson motivation
and job satisfaction. Bagozzi (1980a, 1980b) found that motivation was
positively associated with the industrial salesperson's job satisfaction. Thus,
the more motivated a salesperson is to perform, the more satisfied he or she is
with the job.

Role Perceptions and Job Satisfaction

The relationships between salesperson role conflict *and* ambiguity and job
satisfaction have received substantial research attention. Investigations have

consistently found that as salesperson role conflict increases, job satisfaction is reduced (Aaker and Bagozzi 1979; Bagozzi 1978; Churchill, Ford, and Walker 1976; Dubinsky and Mattson 1979; Dubinsky and Borys 1981; Dubinsky and Skinner 1984a; Franke, Behrman, and Perreault 1982; Mahajan et al. 1984; Teas 1983). Prior research also has generally demonstrated that lower levels of role ambiguity are associated with higher levels of salesperson job satisfaction (Bagozzi 1980b; Berkowitz 1980; Busch and Bush 1978; Churchill, Ford, and Walker 1976; Donnelly and Ivancevich 1975; Dubinsky and Mattson 1979; Dubinsky and Skinner 1984a; Franke, Behrman, and Perreault 1982; Mahajan et al. 1984). Some investigators, though, have found no relationship between role ambiguity and job satisfaction (Bagozzi 1978; Behrmann, Bigoness, and Perreault 1981; Dubinsky and Borys 1981; Teas 1983).

Personal Factors and Job Satisfaction

Certain personal factors may be related to salespeople's job satisfaction. Thus, it may be useful for managers to identify the personal characteristics that are associated with salesperson job satisfaction. If managers can identify these factors, then they can give attention to sales personnel who possess characteristics related to low levels of job satisfaction, and seek to enhance their satisfaction. Despite the intuitive appeal of examining the relationships between personal factors and job satisfaction, few researchers have done so.

Job tenure (length of time in position) has been examined in several job satisfaction studies. These studies have found that job tenure is positively related (Teas 1983), negatively related (Churchill, Ford, and Walker 1976), and generally unrelated (Dubinsky and Borys 1981; Dubinsky and Skinner 1984c; Parasuraman and Futrell 1983; Teas 1980) to salesperson job satisfaction. Education has been determined to be both inversely related (Dubinsky and Skinner 1984c) and generally unrelated (Parasuraman and Futrell 1983) to job satisfaction. Another characteristic, age, was found to be unrelated to job satisfaction (Dubinsky and Skinner 1984c; Parasuraman and Futrell 1983). Income level also has been found to be both positively associated (Parasuraman and Futrell 1983) and inversely associated (Churchill and Pecotich 1982) with job satisfaction, but unrelated to voluntary turnover or withdrawal cognition (indicants of low job satisfaction) (Motowidlo 1983).

Three studies have explored job satisfaction of salesmen and saleswomen, and the findings are again inconsistent. Male and female salespersons have been shown to have comparable levels of job satisfaction (Busch and Bush 1978; Dubinsky and Mattson 1980), but saleswomen have also been shown to have more job satisfaction than their male counterparts (Dubinsky and Skinner 1984c). Self esteem has been found to be positively related (Aaker and Bagozzi 1979) and unrelated (Bagozzi 1978) to job satisfaction. Internality has been determined to be positively related, and number of nights worked inversely associated with job satisfaction (Franke, Behrman, and Perreault 1982). Several other personal factors have been examined in terms of salesperson satisfaction, but not in more than one study. The following single-study variables have been found to be unrelated to job satisfaction: part-time versus full-time job status (Dubinsky and Skinner 1984b), verbal intelligence and other-directedness (Bagozzi 1978), and higher-order need strength (Teas 1981c).

Structural Factors and Job Satisfaction

Several different structural factors have been examined in terms of their association with salesperson satisfaction (see figure 7–1). Ivancevich and Donnelly (1975) found that "flatter" organizations (those with fewer levels) had salespeople with higher levels of job satisfaction (on two of six satisfaction dimensions: actualization and autonomy) than did "taller" organizations. Churchill, Ford, and Walker (1976) found no relationship between the number of departments affecting the salesperson's job and job satisfaction, but did find a generally negative association between degree of innovativeness the sales job required and satisfaction. Futrell and Jenkins (1978) determined that a limited disclosure of the levels of compensation for salespeople tended to augment salesperson job satisfaction. Bagozzi (1978) ascertained that workload was not associated with job satisfaction.

Several researchers have examined job design variables (e.g., variety, autonomy, and job-provided feedback) and their relationships with job satisfaction. Teas (1981c) discovered that autonomy was positively related, but skill variety, task identity, task significance, and job-provided feedback unrelated to industrial salespeople's work satisfaction. Using a similar methodology to Teas's (1981c), Becherer, Morgan, and Richard (1982) found that none of the above job design characteristics was associated with general satisfaction. Employing a retail sales sample, Teas (1981a) discovered that only autonomy tended to be positively related to the job satisfaction of retail sales personnel; task variety, task significance, and job-provided feedback were generally unrelated to six components of job satisfaction. Dubinsky and Skinner (1984a), however, found that retail salespeople's overall job satisfaction was inversely related to task identity, positively related to variety, and unrelated to autonomy and job-provided feedback. Futrell (1979), in a study of pharmaceutical sales personnel, discovered that nine job design factors (e.g., work challenge and opportunity for creativity) were not associated with job satisfaction.

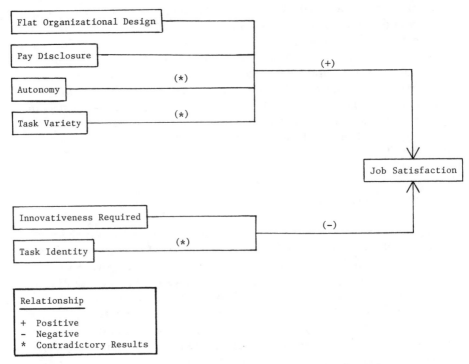

Figure 7–1. Structural Factors and Job Satisfaction

Managerial Actions and Job Satisfaction

Conventional wisdom in sales management suggests that sales managers can affect their salespersons' job satisfaction. Much research has tested this assumption, and many studies have examined the same variables (see figure 7–2).

Several investigations have examined closeness of supervision (or initiation of structure) and its effects on salesperson job satisfaction. The findings show that closeness of supervision is positively related (Churchill, Ford, and Walker 1976; Teas 1980, 1981a) and unrelated (Teas 1983) to job satisfaction. Participation (or salespeople's influence in determining performance standards) also has been explored in many studies, but results are inconsistent. Participation (or influence) has been determined to be generally positively related (Churchill, Ford, and Walker 1976; Teas 1983) and unrelated (Teas 1980, 1981a) to job satisfaction. Managerial feedback has been shown to be positively related (Dubinsky and Borys 1981) and inversely related (Teas 1983) to job satisfaction.

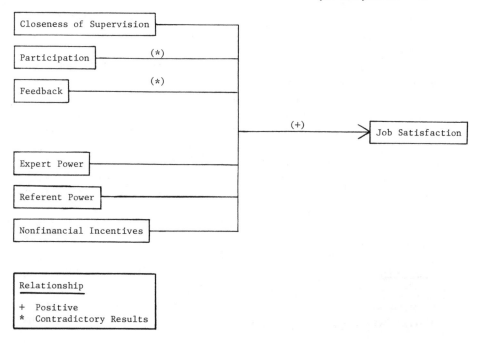

Figure 7–2. Managerial Actions and Job Satisfaction

Some managerial action variables have received attention in only one study. For example, Churchill, Ford, and Walker (1976) found that the amount of communication a manager has with his or her salespeople was generally not associated with job satisfaction. Busch (1980) discovered that the sales manager's use of expert and referent power was consistently related to increased levels of job satisfaction; legitimate, reward, and coercive power did not exhibit such consistency in results. Pruden, Cunningham, and English (1972) examined whether four kinds of nonfinancial incentives (privilege pay, status pay, power pay, and all three combined) were associated with three kinds of job satisfaction (need fulfillment, need deficiencies, or need importance). Their results suggest that salespeople are more satisfied when they receive all three kinds of nonfinancial incentives.

What the Research Suggests

Job satisfaction is important in the sales job because of its potential impact on absenteeism, turnover, and motivation. Because of its significance, researchers have sought factors that are related to it. Based upon our research review, several important conclusions may be drawn concerning salesperson job satisfaction.

Motivated sales personnel appear to have higher job satisfaction than their unmotivated counterparts. This conclusion, however, is based upon only one study, and so is tentative. Nonetheless, managers should seek means of motivating their sales personnel. In chapter 6 we note how this might be done; to summarize: the sales job should be designed to provide salespeople with the opportunities to do a variety of tasks, to complete entire assignments, and to feel their jobs are important to the firm. Also, motivation may be enhanced by managerial encouragement, concern, and awareness for sales personnel and by allowing salespeople to participate in decisions that affect them.

The evidence that role conflict and ambiguity reduce salesperson job satisfaction is overwhelming. Thus, sales managers should attempt to reduce salespeople's role conflict and ambiguity in order to enhance job satisfaction. Role conflict and ambiguity may be reduced, as mentioned in chapter 6, by having sales managers responsible for a relatively small number of salespersons. Also, role ambiguity apparently can be reduced when managers supervise their salespeople closely or allow them to participate in decisions that affect them.

Certain structural (job design) factors appear to have an impact on job satisfaction of sales personnel. In particular, providing job autonomy, whereby salespeople have independence, seems to enhance job satisfaction. Autonomy could be incorporated into the sales job by granting salespeople more discretion in the successful accomplishment of their job. For example, management might allow them to establish their own work assignments and schedules, thus reducing their reliance on management.

Using a limited pay disclosure plan was found (in one study) to enhance job satisfaction. Tentatively, this suggests that such a plan may be implemented successfully. This could be done by articulating to salespeople the following kinds of salary information: range and average earnings of company sales personnel, range and average of annual raises of sales personnel within the firm, and range and average of sales managers' earnings and raises.

Based upon conflicting results, a tentative conclusion is that salespeople's job satisfaction may be enhanced when they are closely supervised and are allowed to participate in key decisions. Thus, sales managers may wish to consider monitoring their salespeople's work closely and being supportive. Moreover, managers may wish to allow salespeople to have meaningful input into decisions that affect their jobs. Such decisions may include establishing quotas, determining discount policies, setting call frequencies and schedules, and ascertaining reimbursable sales-related expenses.

Salesperson job satisfaction may increase when sales managers use expert or referent power. Expert power is demonstrated when managers provide advice and knowledge needed in the salesperson's job. Referent power may be effected through the manager's establishment of warm, interpersonal relationships with the salespeople.

Summary

This chapter reviewed research that focused on how to enhance salespeople's job satisfaction. Motivation, role perceptions, personal factors, structural factors, and managerial actions were discussed in relation to their linkages with job satisfaction. The findings of the studies reviewed indicate that in general job satisfaction is positively related to motivation, autonomy, closeness of supervision, and noncoercive sources of power, but negatively associated with role conflict and ambiguity.

8
Job Performance

This chapter focuses on the major outcome variable of salespeople—job performance (see appendix, table A–8). How salespeople perform their jobs has a major impact on customers, on company management, on salespeople's well-being, and on company viability. Inept salespeople can engender customer ill will, waste precious management time, cause potentially good products to fail in the marketplace, and place undue burdens and constraints on the company. Thus, it is critical that managers strive to generate high levels of performance from their sales personnel. This chapter reviews research that has focused on variables affecting salesperson performance. More specifically, this chapter focuses on the links between salesperson motivation, role perceptions, personal factors, structural factors, managerial actions, and job performance. (See figure 8–1.) The reader should note that, although the studies examined employed a variety of performance measures, regardless of how performance was assessed investigators tended to tap the same basic dimension—job performance.

Motivation and Job Performance

The link between motivation and performance of salespeople has received only scant research attention, although this topic has been extensively investigated by psychologists and organizational behaviorists (e.g., Campbell and Pritchard 1976). Four studies have examined the motivation-performance linkage in a selling context; their findings, however, are not entirely consistent. Bagozzi (1980b) and Oliver (1974) found that salesperson motivation was generally positively associated with performance. Futrell, Parasuraman, and Sager (1983) discovered that effort (one component of motivation) was positively related to performance. On the other hand, Dubinsky and Skinner (1984a), using a sample of retail salespeople, ascertained that motivation was unrelated to performance.

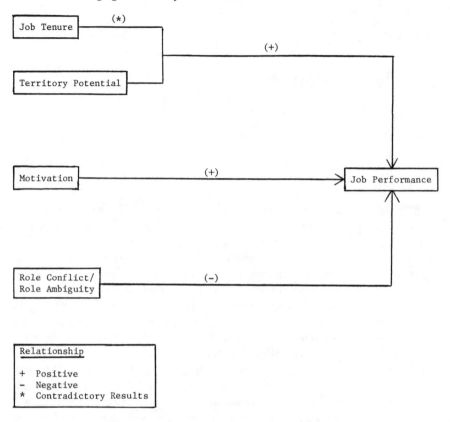

Figure 8–1. Factors Affecting Job Performance

Role Perceptions and Job Performance

When salespeople encounter incompatible demands from their role partners (role conflict), their performance may be impaired because of their inability to satisfy the demands simultaneously. Likewise, when salespeole are unclear or uncertain about how to perform their jobs (role ambiguity), they may execute their tasks inappropriately or fail to execute them at all. As a result, their performance may suffer. Because of the potential effects of salespeople's role perceptions on their performance, much research has been directed toward the role of perceptions–performance linkages.

Findings of prior research generally indicate that salespeople's job performance is lower when role ambiguity (low role clarity) is higher (Bagozzi 1980b; Behrman, Bigoness, and Perreault 1981; Busch and Bush 1978;

Bush and Busch 1981; Dubinsky and Mattson 1979; Dubinsky and Borys 1981; Dubinsky and Skinner 1984a; Franke, Behrman, and Perreault 1982). Bagozzi (1978) and Berkowitz (1980), however, found no relationship between role ambiguity and sales volume of a salesperson. Berkowitz (1980), though, discovered an inverse relationship between role ambiguity and self-rated performance. Prior investigations have found both an inverse association between role conflict (job tension) and performance (Aaker and Bagozzi 1979; Bagozzi 1978; Dubinsky and Mattson 1979) and no relationship between the two (Dubinsky and Borys 1981; Dubinsky and Skinner 1984a; Franke, Behrman, and Perreault 1982).

Personal Factors and Job Performance

If sales managers could identify certain personal characteristics or variables that affect sales performance, then they could focus on the salespeople who possess characteristics associated with lower performance. Management could then seek to augment the performance of such sales personnel. The intuitive appeal of this approach has led several researchers to investigate links between personal factors and salesperson performance.

Some personal factors have been examined in more than one study. Job tenure has been shown to be positively related (Franke, Behrman, and Perreault 1982) and unrelated (Cravens, Finn, and Moncrief 1983) to job performance. Salesperson job satisfaction has been found to be positively associated (Bagozzi 1980a) and unrelated (Dubinsky and Skinner 1984a) to job performance. Task-specific self esteem has been determined to be positively related to performance (Bagozzi 1978, 1980a). Generalized self esteem has been found to be positively related (Bagozzi 1980a) and unrelated (Bagozzi 1978) to performance. Four studies have examined performance differences between salesmen and saleswomen (Busch and Bush 1978; Cravens, Finn, and Moncrief 1983; Dubinsky and Mattson 1980; Swan and Futrell 1978); results of these investigations were inconsistent.

Several other personal factors have been examined, but not in multiple studies. For example, Cravens, Finn, and Moncrief (1983) found that age was unrelated to performance; pay was found to be related to sales but not to percent of quota achieved. Bagozzi (1978) discerned that other-directedness was not associated with performance, but that verbal intelligence was inversely related to performance (Bagozzi 1978, 1980a). Behrman, Bigoness, and Perreault (1981) discovered that salespeople with medium levels of locus of control and low need for clarity had higher levels of performance. Dubinsky and Skinner (1984b) found that full-time sales personnel were better performers than their part-time counterparts. Rafaeli and Klimoski (1983), using a sample of real estate agents and brokers, determined that an individual's handwriting (content of a message) was unrelated to performance. Pruden (1969a) found that salespeople with higher levels of interorganizational linking had higher levels of performance. Small and Rosenberg (1978) examined a set of life history variables (e.g., education, sales aptitude, and marital status) and personality variables (e.g., ascendancy, cautiousness, and personal relations) and discovered that both sets of variables were related to salespeople's performance. Unfortunately, they did not report the specifics of their results.

Structural Factors and Job Performance

Structural factors in relation to salesperson job performance have received a little research interest, but most structural factors have been examined in only one study. Two exceptions are territory potential and workload. Workload has been found to be unrelated to performance in two studies (Bagozzi 1978; Cravens, Finn, and Moncrief 1983). Potential has been shown to be positively related to salesperson sales volume (Bagozzi 1978; Cravens, Finn, and Moncrief 1983) and to percent of sales quota achieved (Cravens, Finn, and Moncrief 1983).

Pruden and Reese (1972) found that to some extent salespeople with more power and authority over company decisions (such as delivery time) performed better than those with less power and authority. Ivancevich and Donnelly (1975) determined that organizational structure (flat, medium, tall) affected efficiency ratings but not absenteeism or route coverage of sales personnel. Darmon (1974) tested the effect of a change in a compensation system on performance and found that, although the average change in performance was zero, individual salespeople experienced sustantial changes in performance (both increases and decreases in performance). Futrell and Jenkins (1978) discovered that where low, medium, and high levels of peer salaries were disclosed, salespeople's performance improved. Futrell, Swan, and Lamb (1977) discovered that the implementation of a management-by-objectives (MBO) program improved the salesperson's performance on eight of ten dimensions. Cravens, Finn, and Moncrief (1983) determined that a company's market share was unrelated to performance. When examining the job design of the retail sales position, Dubinsky and Skinner (1984a) found that autonomy was positively related, but variety, task identity, and job-provided feedback were unrelated to performance.

Managerial Actions and Job Performance

How a manager supervises his or her sales personnel should have an impact on their performance. After all, the nature of the manager–salesperson relationship (e.g., considerate versus hostile, supportive versus destructive, auto-cratic versus democratic) could be either an asset or a liability for salespeople. Despite this logic, only two studies were found that explored the managerial actions–job performance linkages.

Futrell, Swan, and Todd (1976) found very low but significant, positive relationships between ten performance variables and three supervisor clarity/communication-related variables (clarity, influence and control, and perfor-mance-reward variables). Dubinsky and Borys (1981) determined that man-ager-provided feedback was unrelated to performance.

What the Research Suggests

Ultimately, salespeople and their managers are evaluated on how well they perform. Despite marketing scholars' suggestions to assess salesperson per-formance using some measure of profit (e.g., Crissy, Fischer, and Mossman 1973; Kirpalani and Shapiro 1973), recent research suggests that the major-ity of firms continue to judge a salesperson's performance using some kind of sales criterion, such as sales volume obtained or percent of quota achieved (Dubinsky and Barry 1982; Jackson, Keith, and Schlachter 1983). Given this emphasis on production, an important question facing sales managers is, What can be done to enhance sales force productivity? Results from prior investigations of this issue offer several important conclusions.

The research evidence reinforces sales management experience that as salesperson motivation increases, so does performance. The research indi-cates that this is particularly true when nonfinancial incentives are provided to sales personnel. These results suggest that managers should attempt to enhance their salespersons' motivation by designing incentive systems that better meet both the financial and nonfinancial needs of their sales personnel. However, it is not enough to offer desirable and adequate job rewards; sales-people must be able to obtain them and know what they must do to obtain them. This may be done by surveying salespeople's motivational needs and then specifying the contingencies between performance and rewards (instru-mentalities) so that salespeople will know what they must do to obtain the desired rewards.

Sales managers may also seek to enhance salespeople's motivation by designing sales jobs so that they afford salespeople opportunities to perform a variety of critical tasks, complete entire assignments (from beginning to end), and become cognizant that they are an integral part of the firm. In addition, managers should allow sales personnel to participate in decisions that affect their work, and be supportive and show concern and interest in the sales-people and their efforts. Research suggests that such activities can foster salesperson motivation, which in turn enhances performance.

When salespeople experience conflict on the job (role conflict) and are uncertain about how to perform their jobs (role ambiguity), their performance is impaired. Consequently, attempts should be made to resolve salespeople's role conflict and reduce their role ambiguity. To decrease role conflict, the number of salespersons the sales manager supervises (span of control) should not be too great. If this number is too large, the manager will be spread too thin and have inadequate time to spend with the salespeople and help them manage their conflicts. Role ambiguity may also be reduced through limiting the span of control as well as by closely supervising sales personnel to help them clarify their job tasks and responsibilities. Also, allowing salespeople to participate in decisions that affect them will help sales personnel gain an appreciation for, and understanding of, their job assignments—and will provide training for those destined to become managers.

At least at this time, personal factors do not hold promise for sales managers interested in which variables are linked with salesperson performance.

The results concerning structural factors–performance linkages are inconclusive because few structural factors have been consistently studied. However, it appears that certain structural factors may enhance salesperson performance; for example, providing salespeople with adequate job discretion (power, authority, autonomy) tends to improve performance. Also, disclosure of compensation levels for salespeople, on an aggregate basis in terms of range and average of compensation and annual raises, may improve performance. Installation of an MBO program (closely related to the notion of salesperson participation), whereby the manager and salesperson collectively determine the salesperson's goals and strategies to achieve the goals, also appears to offer a means of augmenting performance.

Although one might expect that certain managerial actions would enhance performance of sales personnel, only limited research has focused on this issue. Consequently, suggestions for enhancing performance via managerial actions cannot be offered until further research focuses on the topic.

Summary

This chapter focused on factors that may affect salespeople's performance. Particular attention was paid to motivation, role perceptions, personal factors, structural factors, and managerial actions and their relationships with job performance. Results of the studies reviewed suggest that motivation can enhance performance, but role conflict and ambiguity can impair it. Providing sales personnel with authority also improves performance. Personal factors and managerial actions, to date, have not been demonstrated to have strong association with performance.

Postscript

T his book has reviewed previous research in two areas. First, research studies that attempted to identify characteristics of individuals (e.g., height, weight, aggressiveness) that predict sales success were examined. Particular attention was given to those physical characteristics, mental abilities, personality characteristics, and experience/background factors that have been shown to be related to success in consumer product and service, industrial product and service, insurance, and retail sales. The review of the results of these studies should aid in the recruitment and selection of these four kinds of sales personnel. The second area encompassed studies that attempted to define the factors that affect salespeople's motivation, role perceptions, job satisfaction, and job performance. The purpose of this postscript is to summarize briefly the results of the review of these two areas.

Predictors of Sales Success

Consumer Product and Service Selling

Salespeople with higher levels of intelligence in "high" grade sales positions tend to be more successful in selling consumer products or services than those with lower levels of intelligence. The reverse situation prevails, however, for sales personnel in "low" grade sales positions. Consumer salespeople generally are more successful when they are empathic, extroverted, and genuinely like people. Also, consumer salespeople who demonstrate high levels of aggressiveness, self confidence, and ego drive generally are more successful in their jobs than their counterparts without these characteristics.

Industrial Product and Service Selling

The physical characteristics, mental abilities, personality characteristics, and experience/background factors investigated in previous empirical work apparently are unrelated to success in industrial sales. The lack of substantiated relationships between predictors and sales success may suggest that a "good" industrial salesperson must possess a blend of several important qualities necessary for success rather than one or a few qualities.

Life Insurance Selling

Most investigations that have explored success in life insurance sales generally have not provided clear suggestions for sales recruiters. The research indicates that an agent who is empathic, aggressive, and independent tends to be more successful.

Retail Selling

Although several studies have examined predictors of success in retail sales, the results of these studies are generally unclear about the factors associated with success. Tentatively, we can conclude that retail salespeople who display vigor and have a sense of power are more successful than their counterparts who do not. Physical characteristics, mental abilities, other personality characteristics, and experience/background factors examined in the studies seem to be unrelated to success in retail selling.

Management of Sales Personnel

Part II began with a rather straightforward sales management model (Figure II–1). In it, the relationship of job satisfaction and performance to a salesperson's motivation and role perceptions was portrayed, along with the managerial actions and personal and structural factors affecting both of them. The succeeding three chapters elaborated on the nature and specifics of those interrelationships.

Motivation

Salespeople are generally more motivated when they have opportunities to perform a variety of significant tasks. Moreover, motivation is enhanced when salespeople are able to perform an entire assignment from beginning to end. Salespeople's motivation can also be improved when managers exhibit concern, interest, and awareness toward their sales personnel and allow them to participate in decisions that affect their jobs. Furthermore, motivation of salespeople can be augmented by helping them manage (reduce or alleviate) their job conflicts.

Role Perceptions

Salespeople typically experience role conflict and ambiguity in their jobs, and extreme amounts can affect their performance. Salesperson role conflict and ambiguity are decreased when the number of salespeople their manager supervises (span of control) is reduced. Closely supervising salespeople, allowing them to participate in decisions that affect their jobs, and using expert, legitimate, and referent power may help reduce salesperson role ambiguity.

Job Satisfaction

Research indicates that as salesperson motivation increases, so does job satisfaction. Job satisfaction is also enhanced when sales personnel are provided with some independence and when they are capable of managing their role conflict and ambiguity. Sales personnel who are closely supervised and have input into decisions that affect their jobs exhibit higher levels of job satisfaction than their counterparts who are not closely supervised or allowed to provide input. Job satisfaction can also be increased when the manager employs expert or referent power.

Job Performance

The traditional sales management belief that job performance increases as salesperson motivation increases is supported by research. This enhancement of performance through motivation can be attained by designing sales jobs so that salespeople perform a variety of tasks, complete entire assignments, have job latitude, and feel that they make important contributions to the firm. Furthermore, managers who allow sales personnel to participate in relevant decision making and who show genuine concern and awareness for their sales personnel should have better-performing salespeople. Finally, when role conflict and ambiguity are decreased, job performance of salespeople tends to increase.

Epilogue

Managing a sales force is a difficult task. Sales managers have an abundance of research, however, to assist them in the performance of their duties and responsibilities. This book will help sales managers gain a greater understanding of what research has found concerning predictors of sales success and factors affecting salespeople's motivation, role perceptions, job satisfaction, and job performance. The field of sales management research has come a long way, particularly within the past fifteen years. Much additional work is necessary, however, before more complete and specific guidance on recruitment and selection and management of sales personnel can be provided.

Glossary

Aggressiveness   The extent to which an individual is energetic, vigorous, and action-oriented.

Aspiration level   A measure indicating the extent to which an individual desires to achieve various goals (e.g., move up the corporate hierarchy). *See also* Need for achievement.

Autonomy   A characteristic of a job indicating the extent to which the job provides employees with freedom, independence, and discretion to schedule work assignments and determine the procedures with which to carry them out.

Closeness of supervision   The extent to which a manager supervises employees, monitors their activities, and reduces their job freedom or independence.

Coercive power   The influence an individual has over others, based upon fear; specifically, when subordinates feel that failure to comply with the wishes of their manager may lead to punishment or other negative outcomes (e.g., removal of rewards such as a company car or bonus).

Company relationships   A higher-order reward based on the nature of the interaction (favorable or unfavorable) between an employee and other company personnel. For example, if the work situation allows employees to develop close friendships with fellow employees, company relationships could be considered favorable.

Complexity   A reflection of the number of dimensions of the self that are perceived by the individual. Complex persons are more responsive to others and are more likely to see similarities between themselves and others than are relatively non-complex persons.

Consideration   A leadership style in which managers demonstrate supportive concern, mutual trust, respect, friendliness, and encouragement toward subordinates.

Coworker relation   The nature of the relationships among fellow employees and their perceptions of each other.

Customer dyad   A term that refers to the link between the salesperson and his or her customer.

Direct performance recognition   A higher-order reward that directly acknowledges the employee's performance (e.g., public or private praise from management for a job well done).

Dominance   A personality characteristic of individuals who try to control their environment and to influence or direct other individuals.

Drive   *See* Ego drive.

Earnings opportunity rate   The ratio of a firm's highest-paid salesperson to the average compensation of the sales force. A high ratio may result in salespeople feeling that the compensation program is inequitable, whereas the reverse may be true if the ratio is low.

Effort   A component of motivation. It is the amount of energy or force an individual expends on a given act and is influenced by the individual's needs or motives.

Ego drive   A personality characteristic that indicates the degree to which an individual has the will to achieve, accomplish goals, overcome setbacks, and succeed in endeavors.

Ego involvement   The extent to which individuals receive personal satisfaction from what they do.

Ego strength   A personality construct that indicates the degree to which individuals have been able to achieve a realistic expression of their innate drives.

Emotional control   The extent to which an individual can effectively manage his or her outward emotions.

Empathy   A personality characteristic that refers to the ability of an individual to understand another individual's situation and to view the situation through the eyes of that other person.

Endurance   A personality characteristic that indicates an individual's persistence or tenacity, particularly with respect for work-related activities. It may also be a physiological characteristic.

Esteem (desire for)   A personality characteristic that indicates the extent to which individuals want to be held in high regard by others and are concerned about what others think of them. *See also* Generalized self esteem and Specific self esteem.

Expectancy   A term from Vroom's (1964) motivation theory. It is the perceived probability (estimate) that a given act will be followed by a given outcome. For example, a salesperson might conclude, If I increase my effort (an act) by 20 percent, there is a 40 percent chance (expectancy estimate) that my performance (an outcome) will improve by 20 percent.

Expectancy theory   A motivation theory stating that an individual will select an outcome based upon how the choice relates to some reward. The preferences of the person are based upon the strength of desire to achieve the reward and the perception of the association between the outcome and reward.

Experience/background   Factors that describe an individual's past training, job-related experience, and family background.

Expert power   The ability to influence others because of one's skill, knowledge, or expertise. The less powerful person feels that he or she has less skill, knowledge, or expertise than the more powerful individual.

External orientation   The perspective of individuals who feel that events in their lives are controlled by forces outside of themselves and that they have little control over their lives.

Extrinsic instrumentality   A probability estimate of how likely it is that a particular act (e.g., increasing performance 50 percent) will lead to receipt of an extrinsic job reward (e.g., more pay).

Extrinsic motivation   A form of motivation based upon receiving rewards that are external to the job (e.g., pay, promotion, and fringe benefits).

Extrinsic rewards   Job-related rewards that are not inherent in the job but are external to it (e.g., pay, promotion, and fringe benefits).

Extrinsic valence   The degree of preference an individual has for a particular extrinsic reward (e.g., pay).

Extroversion   A personality characteristic of individuals who are interested in things outside of themselves.

Forcefulness   A personality trait characterized by high levels of dominance, ego drive, self confidence, aggressiveness, and so forth. One of two general kinds of personality characteristics (sociability is the other kind).

Frequency of contact   The extent and regularity with which the manager communicates and interacts with the salesperson via face-to-face meetings, telephone conversations, or written letters or memoranda.

Generalized self esteem   An individual's assessment of overall competence in everyday life and his or her broad feelings of personal regard.

Global instrumentality   An overall assessment of one's instrumentality estimates.

Global self esteem   *See* Generalized self esteem.

Growth   A job reward that offers individuals opportunity to develop and use their skills, abilities, and talents more fully.

Higher-order need strength   The extent to which individuals are motivated (or directed) to work for and attain higher-order rewards (e.g., feelings of accomplishment, personal growth, and liking and respect).

Higher-order rewards   Job rewards that are internal to the job or associated with the job itself, such as the opportunity to perform meaningful work, complete entire assignments, feel challenged, and receive recognition. They are also referred to as intrinsic rewards.

Inclusion   Describes whether or not a working relationship exists between an individual and others (i.e., Do the parties interact?).

Influence in determining standards   The degree to which employees are allowed to provide input into decisions that affect their jobs.

Initiation of structure   A leadership style in which a manager structures and clearly defines the subordinate's role, and thus specifies procedures and assigns tasks and responsibilities.

Instrumentality   A probability estimate of how likely it is that one particular act (e.g., improved job performance) will lead to another act or outcome (e.g., receipt of a reward).

Intelligence   The ability to judge, reason, and deal with abstract ideas and concepts. Intelligence has several dimensions, including arithmetic, mental, social, and verbal.

Interorganizational linking   The extent to which individuals are conduits between their firm and other firms.

Internality   *See* Locus of control.

Internal orientation   The perspective of individuals who feel that they personally control the events in their lives, as opposed to being influenced by outside forces (e.g., family, friends, and supervisors).

Internal work motivation   An indicator of the extent to which an individual is self motivated to perform the job.

Intrinsic instrumentality   A probability estimate of the likelihood that a particular act (e.g., increasing performance by 50 percent) will lead to an intrinsic job reward (e.g., personal growth).

Intrinsic motivation   A form of motivation based upon receiving rewards associated with the job itself (e.g., a sense of accomplishment).

Intrinsic rewards   Rewards related to the job itself, such as the challenge or responsibility of the job, recognition, personal growth, and sense of accomplishment.

Intrinsic valence   An individual's degree of preference for a particular intrinsic reward (e.g., sense of accomplishment).

Introversion   A personality characteristic of individuals who are interested in things directed inward or toward themselves.

Job challenge   The degree to which a job offers employees variety and opportunity to use their skills and abilities.

Job design   The manner in which a job is defined and structured in terms of its variety, autonomy, feedback, task identity, and task significance.

Job importance   The degree to which employees feel that their jobs allow them to make meaningful and significant contributions to the firm.

Job performance   An indicator of how well an individual executes his or her job tasks and responsibilities.

Job-provided feedback   Information about how well one is performing his or her job that is derived directly from the job itself, as opposed to being provided by a manager or peers. For example, salespeople receive job-provided feedback when they receive an order from a customer—an order is part of the job itself.

Job satisfaction   An indicator of the affective reactions (feelings) an individual has toward his or her work situation.

Job significance   *See* Task significance.

Job tenure   The amount of experience the individual has in his or her present position, or in a similar one.

Leader's hierarchical influence   The extent to which employees feel that their supervisor is successful in getting management to recognize employees' problems and successes.

Legitimate power   The ability of an individual to influence others because of his or her position in the firm's hierarchy.

Limited pay disclosure   A compensation plan that provides pay information to employees. For example, the information provided may be the range and average annual earnings of sales personnel, or the range and average of annual raises for sales personnel.

Locus of control   A personality characteristic that indicates people's belief in their ability to influence or control events in their lives. People tend to believe either that events are controlled by themselves (internally oriented) or by forces outside of themselves (externally oriented). *See* External orientation and Internal orientation.

Lower-order rewards   Job rewards that are external to the job, such as pay, benefits, vacation time, and promotion. These are also referred to as extrinsic rewards.

Majority identification   The perception of similarity between oneself and the majority of other individuals, or with more dominant or pervasive individuals.

Management concern and awareness   The degree to which managers assess and react to their employees' needs and problems.

Management by objectives (MBO) A process by which a superior and a subordinate collectively set goals for the subordinate for a given time period and subsequently meet to evaluate the subordinate's performance in relation to the established goals.

Managerial actions A set of managerial behaviors (e.g., providing performance feedback, frequently contacting sales personnel, using referent power) that may affect salespeople's motivation, role perceptions, job satisfaction, and job performance.

Manager-provided feedback Information about how well an employee is performing his or her job that is given by his or her manager.

Manager-rated performance An assessment of an employee's performance made by his or her manager.

Mental abilities The cognitive skills and abilities of an individual (e.g., intelligence, speaking ability, and writing ability).

Motivation An employee's willingness or desire to expend effort on the job.

Need for achievement The degree to which an individual has a drive for accomplishment. A person with a high need for achievement likes to take responsibility and risks, sets moderate goals, and desires feedback about performance.

Need deficiency The degree to which an individual's particular need (e.g., for money) is not satisfied.

Need fulfillment The degree to which an individual's particular need is currently satisfied.

Need importance The degree to which an individual's particular need (e.g., for money) is important to that individual.

Noncoercive power The capacity to influence others through power that is not based on force (referent, expert, or legitimate power), as opposed to coercive power.

Nonfinancial incentives Incentives used to motivate employees that not associated with compensation. Examples include praise, liking and respect, trophies, and plaques.

Organizational identification The extent to which an individual believes that the organization offers an outlet for development and accomplishment of personal skills, goals, and rewards.

Other-directedness A psychological state in which the individual looks to others (as opposed to himself or herself) for direction and guidance. Such individuals tend to be outward oriented.

Participation in decision making *See* Influence in determining standards.

Perceived selling constraints Environmental factors (economic conditions, strength of competition, sales territory potential, and restrictions of product availability) that could hamper the salesperson's performance.

Personal factors Individual characteristics (job experience, education, and so forth) that may be related to salesperson motivation, role perception, job satisfaction, and job performance.

Personality characteristics Psychological factors (sociabilty and forcefulness) that may be related to sales success.

Physical traits Characteristics (generally observable) that may be related to selling success, such as sex, height, and weight.

Position The niche or social status of an individual (or group of individuals) within a social structure.

Power The ability to influence another person's actions or behavior.

Power pay A nonfinancial incentive given to an individual to make his or her job more important to the firm (e.g., the ability to discount).

Privilege pay A nonfinancial incentive given to an individual; the freedom the manager grants subordinates to interact with him or her (e.g., allowing subordinates to act on the same organizational level with the manager).

Promotion opportunity rate The likelihood that a salesperson will be promoted within the year, expressed as a percentage of the sales force promoted during the past year.

Reality distortion The extent to which an individual can psychologically alter his or her perception of a situation to make the situation seem tolerable.

Recognition rate The percentage of the sales force that has been formally recognized for achievement at least once during the past year.

Referent power The ability of one person to influence another individual, based upon the latter's desire to identify with the powerful individual. Thus, the more powerful person is admired because of certain traits or characteristics, and the less powerful individual is influenced by this admiration.

Reward power The ability of one person to influence another individual, based on the latter's hope of receiving rewards from the powerful individual. A less powerful person perceives that compliance with the wishes of the more powerful individual will lead to rewards from the more powerful individual.

Reward valences The degree of an individual's preference for various job rewards.

Role The behavior patterns expected for a particular status position or job.

Role ambiguity A psychological state in which an individual has inadequate knowledge or information with which to perform a job.

Role clarity The degree to which an individual is clear about his or her job responsibilities, tasks, and assignments. High role clarity corresponds to low role ambiguity.

Role conflict A psychological state that occurs when an individual receives incompatible job demands or expectations from two or more parties that cannot be satisfied simultaneously. For example, a customer may want a 10 percent discount from the salesperson, but company management does not permit the salespeople to sell below list price; thus, the salesperson cannot satisfy both the customer and company management and, therefore, experiences role conflict.

Role occupant The individual occupying a particular role in a social structure.

Role overload The degree to which manpower, time, training, or resources provided to an individual are insufficient to complete job assignments.

Role partner A member of an individual's role set who makes demands on or has expectations of the individual. For example, prospective role partners of a salesperson might include the salesperson's manager, customers, fellow employees, and family members.

Role perceptions How an individual perceives his or her role, particularly in relation to role conflict and ambiguity.

Role set The group of individuals (role partners) who make demands on or have expectations of the individual occupying a particular role.

Sales aptitude The innate ability to perform the job that a person brings to his or her sales position. Given a person's understanding of his or her role and motivation to perform, it may be viewed as a constraint on an individual's ability to perform the job.

Self actualization An individual's need to develop fully his or her skills and abilities.

Self assurance A person's degree of self confidence; the extent to which an individual feels effective in dealing with problems.

Self centrality Self orientation as opposed to other orientation, in which a person perceives the social environment largely from an individual viewpoint rather than from the viewpoint of significant others.

Self confidence *See* Self assurance.

Self esteem *See* Generalized self esteem and Specific self esteem.

Self fulfillment *See* Self actualization.

Self interest The inclusion of oneself with others; it is associated with social trust and acceptance of group norms.

Self-rated performance An employee's own assessment of his or her performance.

Skill variety *See* Variety.

Sociability A personality trait characterized by high levels of extroversion, adaptability to social situations, empathy, and so on. One of two general kinds of personality characteristics (forcefulness is the other kind).

Social adaptability The ability to accommodate oneself to various social settings.

Social intelligence One's tact and diplomacy in dealing with others.

Social recognition A personality characteristic that indicates one's desire to be held in high esteem by acquaintances and one's concern about what people think.

Social status An individual's relative position in a social structure.

Sociometric popularity The degree to which an individual feels accepted in a group situation.

Sociophilia A personality characteristic indicating the degree to which an individual likes people.

Sociophobia A personality characteristic indicating the degree to which an individual dislikes people.

Span of control The number of subordinates reporting directly to a supervisor.

Specific self esteem A personality characteristic that indicates the degree to which a person feels that he or she performs well on the job.

Status pay A nonfinancial incentive given to an individual that involves public acknowledgment (praise, recognition) of the value management places on the individual.

Strategy formulation ability The capacity of the salesperson to analyze his or her impression of the customer and to develop a communication strategy directed at eliciting a favorable response from the customer.

Structural factors A set of organizational (e.g., job design) and environmental (e.g., workload, nature of competition) factors that may affect motivation, role perceptions, job satisfaction, and job performance of sales personnel.

Task autonomy *See* Autonomy.

Task clarity *See* Role clarity.

Task completeness *See* Task identity.

Task complexity *See* Variety.

Task conflict *See* Role conflict.

Task identity A job characteristic that indicates the extent to which the job involves completing an entire and identifiable piece of work—doing a job from beginning to end. For example, a salesperson's job would be high on task identity if he or she identifies prospects, approaches them, makes sales presentations, handles their objections, closes their sale, and services them after the sale is made.

Task significance   *See* Job importance.

Task-specific self esteem   *See* Specific self esteem.

Territory potential   The highest possible amount of industry sales in a salesperson's territory.

Task variety   *See* Variety.

Valence   The degree of an individual's preference for a particular outcome (e.g., job reward).

Variety   A job characteristic that indicates the extent to which a job involves using a variety of different skills and activities to execute tasks and assignments.

Verbal intelligence   An individual's cognitive ability to accurately perceive, attend to, and process information.

Vigor   A form of motivation.

Vocational decisiveness   Purposefulness in selecting an occupation and achieving the necessary qualifications, followed by an early start in the selected occupation.

Vocational maturity   An indicator of the degree of career development of an individual at a particular point in time.

Voluntary turnover   An employee leaving the firm at his or her own discretion (i.e., not terminated by the firm).

Withdrawal cognition   A psychological state corresponding to the frequency with which an employee thinks about quitting the job and his or her intention to quit the job.

Workload   The number of accounts in a salesperson's territory.

Appendix
Tabular Description of
Studies Reviewed

None of the textual material describes the studies reviewed in terms of their methodologies, data analysis techniques, or numeric results. This information is presented in tables A–1 through A–8, which show the nature and size of the sample employed in a particular study; the criterion and predictor variables investigated and the scales used to measure them; and the statistical technique(s) utilized and the results of the data analysis.

A key for the symbols used in tables A–1 through A–8 precedes the tables. Tables A–1 through A–4 portray results of investigations focusing on predictors of sales success. Table A–1 presents the results of studies examining predictors of success in consumer product and service sales; table A–2, results for industrial product and service sales; table A–3, results for life insurance sales; and table A–4, results for retail sales. Tables A–5 through A–8 give findings from studies focusing on salesperson motivation, role perceptions, job satisfaction, and job performance. Table A–5 presents findings of investigations exploring salesperson motivation; table A–6, findings for role perceptions; table A–7, findings for job satisfaction; table A–8, findings for job performance.

Key for Symbols in Tables A–1 Through A–8

Symbol	Technique
*	Significant at $p \leq .05$
NR	Not reported scale or analysis technique used
NS	Not significant $(p > .05)$
(ANOVA)	Analysis of variance
(C.M.:L)	Causal modeling methodology using LISREL analysis package
(CORR)	Pearson Correlation Coefficient
(CTA)	Contingency table analysis
(DIS)	Discriminant analysis
(KS)	Kolmogorov-Smirnov
(MANOVA)	Multiple analysis of variance
(P.A.)	Path analysis
(REGR)	Multiple regression. Only those predictor variables listed where $p \leq .05$.
(S)	Spearman rank order
(S.E.M.)	Structural equation models
(SDS)	Comparison of simple descriptive statistics
(χ)	Chi square
(Z)	Z test of differences

Table A–1
Consumer Product and Service Sales

Situation (Sample Size)	Author (Year)	Criterion Variable (Measurement)	Predictor Variable (Measurement)	(Technique) Strength
Automobiles (n=32) (two firms A, B)	Tobolski & Kerr (1952)	Sales ratio (sales/attempts)	Empathy (Kerr 1951)	(Z) (.44)
				A .42 B .75
		new car		.42 .75
		used car		.05 .18
		Sales manager rating (sales/attempts)	Empathy	(.71)*
		new car		.50 1.0
		used car		.13 .20
Multiple Products	Austin (1954)	Sales ability (author criteria multiple studies)	Intelligence (multiple measures)	
			"low" grades of selling	(−)
			"medium" grades of selling	(0)
			"high" grades of selling	(+)
General (3M) Trade (n=120)	Dunnette & Kirchner (1960)	Manager rating (author scale)	Dominance (Edwards Personal Preference Scale: EPPS)	(CORR) .32*
			(Strong Vocational Interest Blank: SVIB, Witkin 1956)	
			aviator	(−)
			printer	(−)
			math teacher	(−)
			industrial arts teacher	(−)
			forest service man	(−)
			accountant	+
			sales manager	+
			life insurance salesman	
			EPPS—14 subscales	NS
			SVIB—40 subscales	NS

Table A-1 (continued)

Situation (Sample Size)	Author (Year)	Criterion Variable (Measurement)	Predictor Variable (Measurement)	(Technique) Strength
Petroleum (n = 21)	Harrell (1960)	Sales (dollars)		(SDS)
			Mental ability (OTIS)	+
			Bernreuter Personality	
			Stability	+
			Dominance	+
			Self confidence	+
			Agression and drive	+
			Social intelligence (Moss, Hunt, Omwake Tact & Diplomacy)	+
			Vocational: sales manager	+
		Field review (author scale)		
			Sense of humor	+
			Sales sense	+
			(None of previous variables "significantly" related)	NS
		Company appraisal		
			Mental ability (OTIS)	+
			(No other variables "significantly" related)	
			Self-sufficiency	NS
			Social	NS
			Objective-mindedness	NS
			Tact and diplomacy	NS
			Judging behavior	NS
			Sizing people up	NS
			SVIS-8 subcycles	NS
			Canfield Sales Sense Test	NS
			Washburn Social Adjustment Inventory	NS
Petroleum products (n = 65)	Miner (1962)	Sales (high/low)	Intelligence (WAIS) (oral arithmetic)	(CORR) .33 .38

Sample	Author (Year)	Criterion	Predictor / Measure	Result

		Successful performance	Picture Arrangement Test
			  dependence
			  sociophilia
			  self confidence
			  happiness
				.58

		Poor performance	low aggression sociophobia strong superego	
			Overconformity	NS
			Terman Concept Mastery Test	NS
			survey of mechanical insight	NS
			attitude toward job	NS
			intelligence–total score and four subscores	NS
			Weisman Personnel Classification test (WCPT)	NS
			Kuder Preference Record-11 subscales	NS
			Deviance	NS
Auto sales (n = 237)	Greenberg & Mayer (1964)	Sales	Empathy/ego drive (author scale: "multiple personal inventory")	(CORR) .69
Mutual funds (n = 68)	Mayer & Greenberg (1964)	Sales	Empathy/ego drive	.73
Food mfr. (route salespeople) (n = 210)	Baehr & Williams (1968)	Annual number of sales	Manager performance rating	(CORR) .37
		Manager performance rating (R = .42) (author scale) (# statistical significance not reported)	Financial responsibility Leadership group participation Vocational family adjustment Parental family adjustment	(REGR) .33 .14 .06 -.08

Table A–1 (continued)

Situation (Sample Size)	Author (Year)	Criterion Variable (Measurement)	Predictor Variable (Measurement)	(Technique) Strength
		Mean sales volume rank (R = .50)	Early family responsibility	.18
			School achievement	-.05
			Selling experience (Baehr and Williams 1967 scale)	NS
			Financial responsibility	.43*
			Stability	.39*
			General health	-.05
			Higher educational achievement	.12
			School achievement	-.08
		Maximum sales volume rank (R = .36)	Financial responsibility	.31*
			Stability	.27*
			Parental family adjustment	-.11
			Early family responsibility	.17
		Tenure as salesperson (number of years with firm) (R = .30)	Vocational satisfaction	-.18
			Early family responsibility	-.18
			Vocational decisiveness	.12
			School activities	NS
			Vocational decisiveness	NS
			Professional successful parents	NS
		Route difficulty (author scale) (R = .27)	Educational/vocational consistency	.12
			Early family responsibility	-.09
			General health	-.11
			Drive	.16
Truck jobber perishables (n = 172)	Howells (1968)	Manager rating (author scale NR)	(Personal interview, open end question, and observation)	(X)
			Ego involvement	+*
			Primary type (extrovert)	+*
			(Primary type with higher ego involvement)	+*

Sample	Author	Criterion	Variable	(CORR)
Hardware to retailers (n = 120)		Manager rating	Secondary type (introversion)	+*
			(Secondary type with higher ego involvement)	
			Higher ego involvement	+*
				NS
Bulk commodities (n = 118)		Manager rating	Secondary type (introvert)	+*
			(Secondary type with higher ego involvement)	
			Higher ego involvement	+*
				+*
Stocks (n = 81)	Ghiselli (1969)	Tenure (more than three years on job)	Author scale	(CORR)
			Supervisory ability	.53*
			Achievement motivation	.40*
			Intelligence	.38*
			Self assurance	.29*
			Decisiveness	.22*
			Need for self-actualization	.26*
			Need for job security	-.43*
			Need for power over others (i.e. no hard sell)	-.16
			Need for higher financial reward	-.18
			Initiative	.14
Industrial (n > 500, usually)	Ghiselli (1973)	No criterion variable identified by author. Author indicated no test validity established for these results (p. 470)	Intellectual abilities	
			intelligence	.33
			arithmetic	.34
				.29
			Abilities	
			spatial relations	.20
			mechanical principles	.20
			Perceptual accuracy	.16
			number comparison	.23
			name comparison	.27
			Motor abilities	.19
			tapping	.16
			finger dexterity	.17
			hand dexterity	.18
				.13

Table A–1 *(continued)*

Situation (Sample Size)	Author (Year)	Criterion Variable (Measurement)	Predictor Variable (Measurement)	(Technique) Strength
Real estate (n = 87)	Scheibelhut & Albaum (1973)	Sales commission (R = .249)	Personality traits personality interest	.30 .29 .31 (REGR)
			Majority identification	−.278*
			Complexity	.249*
			Self esteem	.057
			Social interest	−.023
			Self centrality	−.014
			Inclusion	.151
				(DIS)
				H L
Appliance wholesaler (n = 19)	Mattheiss et al. (1974)	Manager rating of salespeople into high (H) and low (L) performance categories (criteria unknown)	Occupational level (aspiration)	1.1 1.3
			Supervisory ability	−1.0 1.1
			Self assurance	.9 −1.1
			Intelligence	NS
			Initiative	NS
			Decision making	NS
			Sociometric popularity (Ghiselli Self-Description Inventory: SDI)	NS
				H L
Food wholesaler (n = 19)		Manager rating of performance	Intelligence	1.6 −1.6
			Decision making	−.9 .9
			Initiative (order taking)	1.1 −1.1
			Other four variables not entered	NS
Food wholesaler (n = 18)		Manager rating	Intelligence	.3 −.4
			Initiative	−.8 .8
			Decision making	.5 −.5
			Other four variables not entered	NS

Table A-2
Industrial Product and Service Sales

Situation (Sample Size)	Author (Year)	Criterion Variable (Measurement)	Predictor Variable (Measurement)	(Technique) Strength
General to distributors and manufacturers (n = 539)	Kirchner et al. (1960)	Manager rating (author scale)	Age <30 30–45 >45	(CORR) NS .26* NS
General to distributors and manufacturers (n = 70)	Dunnette & Kirchner (1960)	Manager rating (author scale)	Dominance: (Edwards Personal Preference Scale) Job categories (SVIB) engineer social science teacher production YMCA secretary banker	(CORR) .29* + + + – –
Office systems agricultural supplies (n = 132)	Howells (1968)	Manager rating (author scale; NR)	Ego involvement Primary traits (extrovert) Ego involvement with primary type (Open-ended interview)	($\bar{X}$) +* +* +*
Utility reps (n = 73)	Scheibelhut & Albaum (1973)	Manager rating and self evaluation (NR)(R = .407)	Self esteem Complexity Inclusion Majority identification Self centrality Social interest	(REGR) .331* .407* –.161 .018 –.004 .127

(continued)

Table A–2 (continued)

Situation (Sample Size)	Author (Year)	Criterion Variable (Measurement)	Predictor Variable (Measurement)	(Technique) Strength
		Sales personnel vs. nonsales personnel (difference scores with sign in direction of sales reps)	Inclusion	NS
			Complexity	NS
			Majority identification	+*
			Self centrality	−*
			Social interest	+*
			Self esteem	+*
				(REGR)
Building materials (n = 71)	Lamont & Lundstrom (1977)	Sales Activity Quota (R = NS)	Personality variables	
			dominance	.098
			endurance	.007
			social recognition	.089
			desire for esteem	
			(Author scale: Personality Research Form-PRF)	
			Personal characteristics	
			age, height, weight	.183
			formal education	.082
			outside activities	.041
			civic and professional organizations	.185
		New business conversion (R = .548)	Social recognition	.252*
			Height	.307*
			Outside activities	.288*
			(All other individual variables listed were found to be not significant)	NS
		Commissions	No individual or grouped variables significant	NS
		Incentive earnings	Height (Probably correlated with new business)	.369*
			(All other variables)	NS

Industrial products
(Two firms: A,
n = 100; B,
n = 59)

Perreault et al.
(1977)

Managerial rating overall
performance

Ego strength	−.285*
Endurance	.234*
(All other individual variables)	NS

Salesmanship skills
(rating by managers)
(R = .477)

Endurance	.297*
Ego strength	−.254*
all other individual variables	NS

Supportive and develop-
mental skills (interpersonal
rating by manager)
(R = .519)

Endurance	.297*
Civic and professional organization member	−.270*
All other individual variables	NS

Technical competence/
territory management
(rating by manager)

All other individual variables	NS

Manager rating (author/company
scale into High, Low)

Firm A

	(DIS)	
	H	L
Extroversion	97.4	96.1*
Dominance	96.5	95.4
Self confidence	94.0	92.7
Social dependence	77.7	24.6
Sales aptitude	94.4	89.6
Mental ability	88.0	83.5*
Vocabulary	76.0	76.2
Social intelligence	64.0	56.0*
Business skills	69.3	63.4
(Scales: NR)		

(continued)

Table A–2 (continued)

Situation (Sample Size)	Author (Year)	Criterion Variable (Measurement)	Predictor Variable (Measurement)	(Technique) Strength
		Manager rating (author/company scale) high-performing reps	*Firm B* *First variable* Vigor Cautiousness Sociability	Positive Relationship
			Second variable Sales comprehension Sense of humor	Positive relationship
Strapping (n = 123)	Bagozzi (1978)	Sales ($R^2 = .54$) (median value from sample I)		(REGR)
			Verbal intelligence (Borgatta 1971)	-12.76^*
			Specific self esteem (author)	24.48^*
			Generalized self esteem (Jackson 1975)	NS
			Other-directedness (Rotter 1966)	NS
			Role ambiguity (author)	NS
			Job tension (author scales)	-9.47^*
			Territory potential ($)	$.07^*$
		($R^2 = .40$) (median value from sample II)	Verbal intelligence (Borgatta 1971)	-12.69^*
			Specific self esteem (author)	9.23^*
			Generalized self esteem (Jackson 1975)	NS
			Other-directedness (Rotter 1966)	NS
			Role ambiguity (author)	NS
			Job tension (author scales)	-9.33^*
			Territory potential ($)	$.151^*$

			(REGR)
Industrial products (n = 58)	Weitz (1978)	Impression formation for	
		Performance	
		Factor scores ($R^2 = .252$)	
		relative performance beliefs	−.40*
		strategy formulation ability	.38*
		importance weights	.08
		change potential	−.10
		Instrument sales (dollars) ($R^2 = .185$)	
		relative performance beliefs	−.38*
		strategy formulation ability	.34*
		importance weights	.02
		change potential	.01
		Ratio instrument sales to quota ($R^2 = .228$)	
		relative performance beliefs	−.47*
		strategy formulation ability	.38*
		importance weights	.08
		change potential	.09
		Oscilloscope sales (dollars) ($R^2 = .243$)	
		relative performance beliefs	−.21
		strategy formulation ability	.35*
		importance weights	.10
		change potential	−.25*
		Oscilloscope sales to quota ($R^2 = .182$)	
		relative performance beliefs	−.26
		strategy formulation ability	.30*
		importance weights	−.05
		change potential	−.19
		National sales manager rating ($R^2 = .018$)	
		relative performance beliefs	−.12
		strategy formulation ability	.00
		importance weights	.05
		change potential	.07
			(CM:L)
Steel strapping (n = 122)	Baggozi (1980a)	Sales (dollars)	
		Verbal intelligence (Borgatta 1971)	−.179

Table A-3
Life Insurance Sales

Situation (Sample Size)	Author (Year)	Criterion Variable (Measurement)	Predictor Variable (Measurement)	(Technique) Strength
n = 346	Baier & Dugan (1957)	Composite objective performance measure (PAR)		(CORR)
			Amount personal life insurance owned (belief in product)	.30
			Product knowledge	+
			Training	+
			Industry specific characteristics	+
n = 522	Merenda & Clarke (1959)	Rating (successful salesperson)		(DIS)
			Personality variable	
			aggressiveness	.13
			sociability	.11
			emotional control	-.15
			social adaptability	-.17
			Personal history variables	
			number of children	.12
			educational level	.10
			monthly living expense	.18
			amount of insurance owned	.17
			age	NS
			marital status	NS
			military status	NS
			eductional expenses earned	NS
			number of organizations	NS
			memberships	NS
			experience	NS
			years at present residence	NS
			unearned income	NS
			debts	NS
			sales courses	NS

Study	n	Dependent variable	Independent variables	Results
Evans (1963)	n = 149 dyads	Sales (yes/no)	wife's employment status	NS
			sales experience	NS
			recreational activities	NS
			number of friends	NS
			number of professional friends	NS
			number of offices held	NS
			Similarity	(SDS) +
			age	Results presented in percentage form
			income	
			height	
			education	
			religion	
			political affiliation	
			smoking habits	
			perceptions of:	
			friendship	
			liking	
			pleasant conversation	
			sales rep seemed to enjoy his job	
Greenberg & Mayer (1964)	n = 127	Sales (dollars)	Empathy	(CORR) +.72*
			Ego strength (Author derived scales: Multiple Personal Inventory)	
Tanofsky et al. (1969)	n = 1,525	Salary	Prior income	(SDS) +
			Number of dependents	+
			Sales experience	NS
			Education	NS
			Marital status	NS
			Age	NS

(continued)

Table A–3 (continued)

Situation (Sample Size)	Author (Year)	Criterion Variable (Measurement)	Predictor Variable (Measurement)	(Technique) Strength
n = 10,111	Brown (1978)	Survival rate (agents operating 1933–1971)	Number of dependents	(CORR) +
			Time with most recent employer	+
			Membership in organizations (number)	+
			Offices held in organizations (number)	+
			Net worth ($)	+
			Minimum current living expenses	+
			Amount of life insurance owned	+

Table A–4
Retail Sales

Situation (Sample Size)	Author (Year)	Criterion Variable (Measurement)	Predictor Variable (Measurement)	(Technique) Strength
General (not specified) (n = 170)	Mosel (1952)	Sales (dollars)		(χ)
			Age	+
			Education	+
			Experience	+
			Marital status	+
			Number of dependents	–
			Time lost on job (2 years)	NS
			Weight	NS
			Height	NS
			Domicile	NS
			Thirty other items	NS
Furniture (n < 25)	French (1960)	Sales (dollars)		(SDS)
			Age	NS
			Experience	NS
			Education	NS
			Social status (NR)	+
			Coworker relation (NR)	–
			Anticipated job mobility (NR)	+
			Job satisfaction (NR)	NS
Appliances (n = 63)	Cotham (1968)	Income ($ commission)		(CORR)
			Vigor	+.30*
			Feelings of personal worth	+.28*
			Pay satisfaction	+.36*
			Pay satisfaction (as compared to other companies)	+.29*
		Income (adjusted for relative store size)	No variables significant	NS

(continued)

Table A–4 (continued)

Situation (Sample Size)	Author (Year)	Criterion Variable (Measurement)	Predictor Variable (Measurement)	(Technique) Strength
		Sales volume (actual sales)	Vigor	+.26
			Pay satisfaction	+.27
		Sales volume (adjusted for relative store size)	Vigor	+.25
			Pay satisfaction	+.27
Appliances (n = 62)	Cotham (1969)	Sales volume achieved		(CORR)
			Age	+.34*
			Club membership	+.33*
			Amount of time wife works	–.30*
			Formal education	+.29*
			Retail selling experience (years)	+.43*
		Sales volume adjusted (different store sizes)	Amount of time wife works	–.28*
			Four other variables	NS
			All five variables not significant	NS
		Manager rating (by department manager of overall performance)	City size lived in prior to age 21	–.28*
			Expected future income	+.25*
			Retail selling experience	+.34*
			Desired job responsibility	NS
			Sibling rank	NS
			Perceived athletic ability	NS
		Manager rating (by store manager of overall performance)	Perceived artistic ability	+.25*
			Desired job responsibility	–.26*
			Expected future income	+.25*
			All other four variables	NS
General (n = 123)	Weaver (1969)	Sales (average daily)		(CORR)
			Age	+.90
			Education (to high school, not college)	+.80

Study	Criterion variables	Predictor variables	
			+
			low?
			+
			(CORR)
Ghiselli (1973) General (n = > 500, generally)	No criterion variables listed	Marital status	
		married/divorced	+
		single/separated	low?
		Perception of power	+
		Intellectual abilities	
		intelligence	−.06
		immediate memory	−.06
		substitution	−.16
		arithmetic	.10
		Spatial and mechanical abilities	
		spatial relations	.14
		mechanical principles	.14
		Perceptual accuracy	−.02
		number comparison	−.14
		name comparison	.00
		cancellation	.02
		Motor abilities	.09
		tapping	.21
		finger dexterity	−.05
		hand dexterity	.11
		Personality traits	.35
		personality	.36
		interest	.34
Churchill et al. (1975) Clothing: men/women (n = 237)	Purchase vs. nonpurchase	Similarity coefficient all education, religion, political, age, height, nationality, race, sex visible similarity: education, age, height, nationality, race, sex	NS
			(REGR)
	Amount of purchase (directional support but not statistically significant)	All characteristics	.02
		Visible characteristics of similarity	.02

(continued)

Table A–4 *(continued)*

Situation (Sample Size)	Author (Year)	Criterion Variable (Measurement)	Predictor Variable (Measurement)	(Technique) Strength
General (n = 768)	Spivey et al. (1979)	Low vs. high risk (tenure, performance [rating], security risk) ($W^2 = .57$)		(DIS)
			Outgoing personality	.48
			Assertiveness	.30
			External (Rotter 1966)	−.30
		Low risk		NR
		(manager rating on: tenure, performance, security risk)		
		high risk		
			Reserved personality (Cattel)	.33
			Shy	.38
			Demographics	
			number of children	−.31
			previous work hours <40 hrs/week	.39
			Life history	
			changed job to do more inventory work	.32
			never wanted something bad enough to do almost anything to get it	.33

Table A–5
Salesperson Motivation

Situation (Sample Size)	Author (Year)	Criterion Variable (Measurement)	Predictor Variable (Measurement)	(Technique) Strength
				(ANOVA)
Industrial products (n = 227; two firms)	Churchill et al. (1979)	Lower order rewards pay (author scale all variables)	Job tenure	3.27*
			Age	1.79
			Marital status	2.57*
			Family size	.84
			Education	.01
		security	Job tenure	2.04
			Age	2.19
			Marital status	.12
			Family size	.83
			Education	1.28
		Higher order rewards recognition	Job tenure	2.01
			Age	.50
			Marital status	.01
			Family size	3.05*
			Education	.01
		promotion	Job tenure	6.78*
			Age	4.31*
			Marital status	.05
			Family size	2.66*
			Education	.41
		liking and respect	Job tenure	.42
			Age	.92
			Marital status	.01
			Family size	.43
			Education	.36

(continued)

Table A-5 (continued)

Situation (Sample Size)	Author (Year)	Criterion Variable (Measurement)	Predictor Variable (Measurement)	(Technique) Strength
		sense of accomplishment	Job tenure	1.19
			Age	2.60*
			Marital status	.15
			Family size	3.38*
			Education	.42
		personal growth	Job tenure	3.36*
			Age	5.00*
			Marital status	.65
			Family size	3.14*
			Education	1.92
		average valence for higher order	Job tenure	6.30*
			Age	7.84*
			Marital status	.18
			Family size	5.90*
			Education	.45
				(CORR)
Pharmaceutical sales (n = 605)	Futrell (1979)	Intrinsic motivation (Porter 1961)	Job design	All NS
			clear on results expected	
			clear on goal importance	
			unclear on superior's opinion	
			influence in setting job goals	
			have little control and final say	
			have control and final say	
			allowed to be creative	
			challenged by work	
			no need to develop new job ideas	
Industrial products/ services (n = 200, four firms)	Doyle & Shapiro (1980)	Motivation (respondent self-report on hours spent per week in selling and/or sales activities)	Type of compensation plan (incentive pay)	(NR)
				+
			Task clarity (higher clarity)	+

			+ (REGR)
		Salesperson achievement need (higher need to achieve) (Author combination of 3–4 psychological scales)	
Tyagi (1980)	Intrinsic rewards (job outcomes) (Jones & James 1977) (R² = .24)	Job challenge and variety	.38*
Insurance (n = 116)		Job importance	.76*
		Leader's hierarchical influence	.32*
		Job autonomy	NS
		Leadership consideration	NS
		Organizational identification	NS
	Extrinsic rewards (job outcomes) (R² = .39)	Job challenge and variety	.44*
		Job importance	.82*
		Leadership consideration	.26*
		Organizational identification	.10
		Job autonomy	NS
		Leader's hierarchical influence	NS
Teas (1981b)	Expectancy (Sims et al. 1976 and author scale) (R² = .526)	Specific self esteem (Bagozzi 1978)	.265*
Industrial (n = 171)		Participation (Hackman & Oldham 1975)	.184*
		Task variety and completeness (Hackman & Oldham 1975)	.123*
		Task complexity (Hackman & Oldham 1975)	.132*
		Perceived selling constraints (author scale)	–.323*
		Global self esteem (Jackson 1975)	NS
		Job experience (number of years in current firm)	NS
		Internal/external orientation (Valecha 1975)	NS

(continued)

Table A–5 (continued)

Situation (Sample Size)	Author (Year)	Criterion Variable (Measurement)	Predictor Variable (Measurement)	(Technique) Strength
			Consideration (House & Dessler 1974)	NS
			Initiation of structure (House & Dessler 1974)	NS
			Performance feedback (Hackman & Oldham 1975)	ND
			Job significance/autonomy (Hackman & Oldham 1975)	NS
		Global instrumentality (author scale) ($R^2 = .489$)		(REGR)
			Internal/external orientation	.096*
			Consideration	.269*
			Participation	1.578*
			Task significance/autonomy	.101*
			Task variety/completeness	.216*
			Initiation of structure and task complexity	1.031*
			Participation and task complexity	-.901*
			Initiation of structure	NS
			Feedback	NS
			Task complexity	NS
			Initiation of structure and participation	NS
Industrial (n = 214)	Becherer et al. (1982)	Internal motivation (all variables measured Hackman & Oldham 1975) ($R^2 = .39$)		(REGR)
			Experienced meaningfulness	.19*
			Experienced responsibility	.36*
			Knowledge of results	.03
			Skill variety	.10*
			Task identity	-.03

Study	Category	Variable	(REGR)
		Task significance	.04
		Autonomy	.06
		Feedback	.01
Teas (1982)	Self-fulfillment ($R^2 = .317$) (all Teas 1981b)	Internal/external orientation	.230*
Retail (n = 93)		Consideration	NS
		Initiation of structure	.183*
		Organizational feedback	NS
		Task variety	.252
		Task significance	.210*
		Task autonomy	NS
		Task feedback	NS
		(Hackman & Oldham 1975; Halpin & Winer 1973; Rotter 1966)	
	Company relationship ($R^2 = .194$)	Internal/external orientation	.239*
		Consideration	NS
		Initiation of structure	NS
		Organizational Feedback	NS
		Task variety	NS
		Task significance	NS
		Task autonomy	NS
		Task feedback	NS
	Growth ($R^2 = .259$)	Internal/external orientation	.259*
		Consideration	.326*
		Initiation of structure	NS
		Organizational feedback	NS
		Task variety	NS
		Task significance	NS
		Task autonomy	NS
		Task feedback	.195*
	Direct performance recognition ($R^2 = .396$)	Internal/external orientation	.241*
		Consideration	.321*
		Initiation of structure	NS

(continued)

Table A–5 (continued)

Situation (Sample Size)	Author (Year)	Criterion Variable (Measurement)	Predictor Variable (Measurement)	(Technique) Strength
				(REGR)
			Organizational feedback	.240*
			Task variety	NS
			Task significance	NS
			Task autonomy	NS
			Task feedback	NS
Insurance (n = 104)	Tyagi (1982)	Expectancy scores (author scale) ($R^2 = .294$)	Job challenge and variety	.04
			Job importance	.12
			Task conflict	−.33*
			Role overload	−.02
			Leadership consideration	.29*
			Organizational identification	.28*
			Management concern and awareness	.26*
		Intrinsic instrumentality (author scale) ($R^2 = .337$)	Job challenge and variety	.09
			Job importance	.27*
			Task conflict	−.33*
			Role overload	−.35*
			Leadership consideration	.27*
			Organizational identification	.37*
			Management concern and awareness	.24*
		Extrinsic instrumentality ($R^2 = .16$)	Job challenge and variety	.16
			Job importance	.21*
			Task conflict	.01
			Role overload	.02
			Leadership consideration	.24*
			Organizational identification	.08
			Management concern and awareness	.06

Intrinsic motivation ($R^2 = .360$)	Job challenge and variety	.02
	Job importance	.26*
	Task conflict	−.33*
	Role overload	−.23*
	Leadership consideration	.38
	Organizational identification	.45*
	Management concern and awareness	.38*
Extrinsic motivation ($R^2 = .19$)	Job challenge and variety	.06
	Job importance	.29*
	Task conflict	−.27*
	Role overload	−.07
	Leadership consideration	.05
	Organizational identification	.26*
	Management concern and awareness	.07
Intrinsic valence (author scale) ($R^2 = .297$)	Job challenge and variety	.19*
	Job importance	.21*
	Task conflict	−.01
	Role overload	.00
	Leadership consideration	.00
	Organizational identification	.34*
	Management concern and awareness	.27*
Extrinsic valence ($R^2 = .42$)	Job challenge and variety	.36*
	Job importance	.38*
	Task conflict	−.26*
	Role overload	−.05
	Leadership consideration	.22*
	Organizational identification	.01
	Management concern and awareness	.02
		(CORR/ANOVA)
Increased pay	Personal characteristics	
	age	NS
	job tenure	NS
	family size	NS

Ingram & Bellenger (1983)

Industrial (n = 241)

(continued)

Table A–5 (continued)

Situation (Sample Size)	Author (Year)	Criterion Variable (Measurement)	Predictor Variable (Measurement)	(Technique) Strength
			educational level	NS
			income level	NS
			vocational maturity	NS
			specific self esteem (Bagozzi 1980b; Zelkowitz 1980b)	
		Increased job security	age	NS
			job tenure	NS
			family size	NS
			educational level	-.135*
			income level	NS
			vocational maturity	NS
			specific self esteem	NS
		Increased recognition	age	NS
			job tenure	NS
			family size	NS
			educational level	NS
			income level	-.126*
			vocational maturity	NS
			specific self esteem	NS
		Promotion	age	NS
			job tenure	NS
			family size	NS
			educational level	NS
			income level	NS
			vocational maturity	NS
			specific self esteem	NS
		Liking and respect	age	NS
			job tenure	NS
			family size	NS
			educational level	NS

	income level	NS
	vocational maturity	NS
	specific self esteem	−.118*
Sense of accomplishment	age	NS
	job tenure	NS
	family size	NS
	educational level	NS
	income level	NS
	vocational maturity	NS
	specific self esteem	NS
Increased personal growth	age	NS
	job tenure	NS
	family size	NS
	educational level	NS
	income level	NS
	vocational maturity	NS
	specific self esteem	NS
Increased pay	Organizational characteristics	
	commission based plan	NS
	promotion opportunity rate	.177*
	recognition rate	.145*
	earnings opportunity rate	NS
Increased job security	salary-based plan	NS
	promotion opportunity rate	−.158*
	recognition rate	.123*
	earnings opportunity rate	NS
Increased recognition	salary-based plan	NS
	promotion opportunity rate	NS
	recognition rate	NS
	earnings opportunity rate	NS
Promotion	salary-based plan	NS
	promotion opportunity rate	−.184
	recognition rate	NS
	earnings opportunity rate	NS

(continued)

Table A–5 (continued)

Situation (Sample Size)	Author (Year)	Criterion Variable (Measurement)	Predictor Variable (Measurement)	(Technique) Strength
		Liking and respect	salary-based plan	NS
			promotion opportunity rate	-.163*
			recognition rate	.118*
			earnings opportunity rate	NS
		Sense of accomplishment	salary-based plan	NS
			promotion opportunity rate	-.123*
			recognition rate	NS
			earnings opportunity rate	NS
		Increased personal growth	commission-based plan	6.23*
			promotion opportunity rate	NS
			recognition rate	NS
			earnings opportunity rate	NS
Retail (n = 116)	Dubinsky & Skinner (1984a)	Work motivation (Hackman & Oldham 1975)	Variety	(P.A.) .235*
			Task identity	.262*
			Role ambiguity	-.266*
			Autonomy	NS
			Feedback	NS
			Role conflict (Hackman & Oldham 1975; Rizzo et al. 1970)	NS
Retail (n = 116)	Dubinsky & Skinner (1984b)	Internal work motivation (Hackman & Oldham 1975)	Job status	(ANOVA) Part Time 32.30 / Full Time 34.08 NS

Table A–6
Salesperson Role Perceptions

Situation (Sample Size)	Author (Year)	Criterion Variable (Measurement)	Predictor Variable (Measurement)	(Technique) Strength
Industrial equipment (n = 265, ten companies)	Walker et al. (1975)	Role conflict (Churchill et al. 1974)		(CORR)
			Number of organization departments affecting activities	−.017
			Closeness of supervision	−.018
			Influence in determining standards by which supervised	.006
			Innovativeness	.011
			Frequency of contact	−.038
			Time in position	−.123*
		Role conflict (R² = .151)		(REGR)
			Number of organization departments affecting activities	−.029
			Closeness of supervision	−.022
			Influence in determining standards by which supervised	.010
			Innovativeness	.030
			Frequency of contact	−.069
			Time in position	−.153*
		Role ambiguity (Churchill et al. 1974)		(CORR)
			Number of organization departments affecting activities	.039
			Closeness of supervision	−.189*
			Influence in determining standards by which supervised	−.069
			Innovativeness	.010
			Frequency of contact	−.011
			Time in position	−.117*

(continued)

Table A–6 (continued)

Situation (Sample Size)	Author (Year)	Criterion Variable (Measurement)	Predictor Variable (Measurement)	(Technique) Strength
		Role ambiguity (R^2 = .363)		(REGR)
			Number of organization departments affecting activities	.060
			Closeness of supervision	-.235
			Influence in determining standards by which supervised	-.267*
			Innovativeness	.033
			Frequency of contact	-.015
			Time in position	-.139*
Pharmaceutical (n = 78)	Busch & Bush (1978)	Role clarity (Donnelly & Ivancevich 1975)	Sex	(Z) Male Female 20.82* 18.10
Industrial (n = 107)	Teas et al. (1979)	Role clarity (Rizzo et al. 1970) (R^2 = .460)		(REGR)
			Performance feedback (Sims et al. 1976)	.517*
			Participation (Vroom 1963)	232
Pharmaceutical sales (n = 415, three companies)	Busch (1980)	Role clarity (author scale)		(CORR)
			Firm 1 (n = 159)	
			expert	.46*
			referent	.24*
			legitimate	.11
			reward	-.11
			coercive	-.05
			Firm 2 (n = 128)	
			expert	.02
			referent	.24*
			legitimate	.25*
			reward	.08
			coercive	-.01*

Setting	Author	Variables	Independent variables	Results
Retail (n = 203)	Dubinsky & Mattson (1980)	Role conflict, role ambiguity, (author scales)	Firm 3 (n = 128) expert referent legitimate reward coercive (All scales, author modified Burke & Wilcox 1971)	.21* .12 .15* −.05 −.13*
Pharmaceutical sales (n = 437, three firms)	Bush & Busch (1981)	Role clarity (Donnelly & Ivancevich 1975)	Sex Age (years)	(CORR) NS NS
Retail (n = 203)	Dubinsky & Borys (1981)	Role ambiguity (author scale) ($R^2 = .22$) Role conflict (author scale) ($R^2 = .05$)	Performance feedback (author scale) Job experience Performance feedback (author scale) Job experience	(REGR) −.387* −.229* (REGR) −.187* .147*
Industrial (n = 122)	Chonko (1982)	Role conflict (Rizzo et al. 1970, Ford et al. 1975, author scales) Role ambiguity (same)	Span of control (number of reps reporting to manager) Span of control	(S) .86* .87*
Industrial (n = 116)	Teas (1983)	Role conflict ($R^2 = .26$)	Consideration Initiation of structure Participation Feedback Experience	(REGR) −.379* .195* −.155* NS NS

(Z)
Male   Female
Both   NS

(continued)

Table A–6 (continued)

Situation (Sample Size)	Author (Year)	Criterion Variable (Measurement)	Predictor Variable (Measurement)	(Technique) Strength
		Role ambiguity (Rizzo et al. 1970) ($R^2 = .34$)	Consideration Feedback Participation Initiation of structure Experience (All Hackman & Oldham 1975; House & Dessler 1974)	$-.288^*$ $-.184^*$ $-.261^*$ NS NS
Retail (n = 116)	Dubinsky & Skinner (1984a)	Role conflict ($R^2 = .11$)	Autonomy Feedback Variety Task identity	(P.A.) $-.208^*$ $-.185^*$ NS NS
		Role ambiguity (Rizzo et al. 1970) ($R^2 = .11$)	Autonomy Task identity Variety Feedback (Sims et al. 1976)	$-.177^*$ $-.209^*$ NS NS
Retail (n = 157)	Dubinsky & Skinner (1984c)	Role conflict	Job status	(ANOVA) Part Time / Full Time 28.14 29.08 NS
		Role ambiguity (Rizzo et al. 1970)	Job status	14.28 12.25 NS

Table A–7
Salesperson Job Satisfaction

Situation (Sample Size)	Author (Year)	Criterion Variable (Measurement)	Predictor Variable (Measurement)	(Technique) Strength
				(S)
Building materials (12 = 100)	Pruden et al. (1972)	Job satisfaction (Tansky 1963) need fulfillment	Privilege pay	NS
			Status pay	NS
			Power pay	.25*
			Combined	.24*
		need deficiencies	Privilege pay	NS
			Status pay	−.22*
			Power pay	−.23*
			Combined	−.31*
		need importance	Privilege pay	NS
			Status pay	NS
			Power pay	NS
			Combined	NS
			(Dubin 1958)	
				(CORR)
Industrial (n = 86)	Donnelly & Ivancevich (1975)	Job satisfaction (author scale) autonomy esteem self actualization	Role clarity (author scale)	.61* .54* .38*
				(ANOVA)
Trade selling to retailer (n = 295, three companies)	Ivancevich & Donnelly (1975)	Job satisfaction (author scale) self-actualization	Tall organization	3.71*
			Medium organization	3.85*
			Flat organization	4.84*
			(Berry & Sadler 1967)	
		autonomy	Tall organization	3.90*
			Medium organization	4.01*
			Flat organization	4.59*

(continued)

Table A–7 (continued)

Situation (Sample Size)	Author (Year)	Criterion Variable (Measurement)	Predictor Variable (Measurement)	(Technique) Strength
		innovativeness	Tall organization	3.98
			Medium organization	4.00
			Flat organization	4.13
		social interaction	Tall organization	4.12
			Medium organization	3.94
			Flat organization	3.99
		security	Tall organization	4.19
			Medium organization	4.33
			Flat organization	4.41
		pay	Tall organization	4.39
			Medium organization	4.64
			Flat organization	4.58
		Anxiety stress (Indik et al. 1964)	Tall organization	2.98*
			Medium organization	3.01*
			Flat organization	1.70*
				(REGR)
Industrial equipment (n = 265, ten companies)	Churchill et al. (1976)	Total job satisfaction (Churchill et al. 1974) ($R^2 = .424$)	Closeness of supervision	.282*
			Influence over standards	.408*
			Amount of communication	NS
			Number of departments	NS
			Innovativeness	−.154*
			Role ambiguity	−.192*
			Role conflict	−.256*
			Time in position	−.828*
		Job itself ($R^2 = .187$)	Closeness of supervision	.186*
			Influence over standards	.273*
			Role ambiguity	−.188*
			Time in position	−.738*
		Fellow workers ($R^2 = .112$)	Influence over standards	.229*
			Role ambiguity	−.193*

Study	Construct	Variable	Coefficient
	Supervision ($R^2 = .332$)	Closeness of supervision	.458*
		Influence over standards	.319*
		Innovativeness	−.202*
		Role conflict	−.116*
	Company policies and support ($R^2 = .324$)	Closeness of supervision	.208*
		Influence over standards	.328*
		Innovativeness	−.118*
		Role ambiguity	−.157*
		Role conflict	−.322*
	Pay ($R^2 = .193$)	Influence over standards	−.203*
		Amount of communication	.320*
		Role ambiguity	−.157*
		Time in position	−.112*
	Promotion and advancement ($R^2 = .292$)	Closeness of supervision	.169*
		Influence over standards	.351*
		Innovativeness	−.109*
		Role conflict	−.281*
		Time in position	−.715*
	Customers ($R^2 = .183$)	Amount of communication	−.690*
		Role ambiguity	−.378*
		Role conflict	−.111*
Steel strapping (n = 161) Bagozzi (1978)	Job satisfaction (Pruden & Reese 1972, and author items) ($R^2 = .27$)	Job tension (role conflict: Kahn et al. 1970)	(REGR) −.442*
		Job performance (dollar volume sales one year)	.003
	(Smallest of six regression runs)	Self esteem: specific and general	NS
		Role ambiguity	NS
		Territory workload	NS
		Verbal intelligence	NS
		Other-directedness	NS

(continued)

Table A–7 (continued)

Situation (Sample Size)	Author (Year)	Criterion Variable (Measurement)	Predictor Variable (Measurement)	(Technique) Strength	
				(CORR)	
Pharmaceutical (n = 78)	Busch & Bush (1978)	Satisfaction (Smith et al. 1969, plus author scale)	Role clarity (Donnelly & Ivancevich 1975)		
		work		.41*	.59*
		supervision		.30*	.27*
		customer		—	.64*
		promotion		.28*	—
		Propensity to leave (Donnelly & Ivancevich 1975)	Role clarity	−.30*	−.43*
				(Z)	
		Job satisfaction (Smith et al. 1969)	Sex	*Male*	*Female*
		coworkers		NS	
		supervisors		NS	
		customers		NS	
		work		NS	
		pay		NS	
		promotion		NS	
				(ANOVA)	
Pharmaceutical (n = 508)	Futrell & Jenkins (1978)	Job satisfaction	Pay disclosure vs. secrecy (Signs in direction of disclosure)		
		pay		+	*
		promotion		+	*
		superiors		−	*
		work		+	*
		coworkers			NS
				(S.E.M.)	
Steel strapping (n = 106)	Aaker & Bagozzi (1979)	Job satisfaction (author scale)	Job performance (dollar sales)	.06*	
			Job tension (role conflict) (Kahn et al. 1964)	−.60*	
			Self esteem (author scale)	.19*	

				(CORR)
Retail (n = 203)	Dubinsky & Mattson (1979)	Overall job satisfaction (author modified, Donnelly & Ivancevich 1975)	Role conflict Role ambiguity (author scales)	−.15* −.25*
		Organizational commitment (author modified, Donnelly & Ivancevich 1975)	Role conflict Role ambiguity	−.12* −.31*
				(CORR)
Pharmaceutical sales (n = 605)	Futrell (1979)	Involvement (Lodahl & Kejner 1965)	Job design (Futrell et al. 1976) clear on results expected clear on goal importance unclear on superior's opinion influence in setting job goals have little control and final say allowed to be creative challenged by work no need to develop new job ideas	.18* .10* NS NS NS NS NS NS NS
		Job satisfaction (author scale)	Job design factors previously listed Job behavior ability to increase work output extent seeking another job	NS NS NS
				(C.M.:L)
Steel strapping (n = 122)	Bagozzi (1980a)	Job satisfaction (author scale)	Performance (dollar sales) Achievement motivation (combination of two author scales)	.308* .519*
				(C.M.:L)
Steel strapping (n = 122)	Bagozzi (1980b)	Job satisfaction (author scale)	Motivation (Duncan 1969) Role ambiguity (Kahn et al. 1964)	.478* −.229*
		Self esteem (author scale)	Motivation Role ambiguity	.347* −.528*

(continued)

Table A–7 (continued)

Situation (Sample Size)	Author (Year)	Criterion Variable (Measurement)	Predictor Variable (Measurement)	(Technique) Strength
				(CORR)
Industrial chemicals (n = 148)	Berkowitz (1980)	Job satisfaction	Role clarity (Donnelly & Ivancevich 1975)	.49*
			Role strain	−.33*
Pharmaceutical sales (n = 415, three firms)	Busch (1980)	Satisfaction with supervision (Smith et al. 1969)	Firm 1 (n = 159)	
			expert power	.69*
			referent power	.58*
			legitimate power	.08*
			reward power	.03
			coercive power	−.22*
			Firm 2 (n = 128)	
			expert	.48*
			referent	.50*
			legitimate	−.05
			reward	−.01
			coercive	−.03
			Firm 3 (n = 128)	
			expert	.58*
			referent	.45*
			legitimate	.25*
			reward	.22*
			coercive	−.21*
			(author modified Burke & Wilcox 1971)	
		Propensity to leave (Donnelly & Ivancevich 1975)	Firm 1 (n = 159)	
			expert	−.31*
			referent	−.25*
			legitimate	−.16*
			reward	.08
			coercive	.03

Study	Sample	Dependent variable	Independent variable	Male	Female
					(Z)
				22.04	22.55
Dubinsky & Mattson (1980)	Retail (n = 203)	Overall job satisfaction (author scale)	Sex		NS
			Firm 2 (n = 128)		
			expert		−.35*
			referent		−.19*
			legitimate		−.14*
			reward		−.10
			coercive		.01
			Firm 3 (n = 128)		
			expert		−.17*
			referent		−.09
			legitimate		−.05
			reward		−.11
			coercive		.02
Teas (1980)	Industrial (n = 127)	Extrinsic job satisfaction (author modified, Porter and Lawler 1968) (R^2 = .279)	Closeness of supervision with indirect role ambiguity influence (Halpin & Winer 1957)		(REGR) .341*
			Participation (modified Vroom 1963)		NS
			Experience (years with company)		NS
		Intrinsic job satisfaction (modified Porter & Lawler 1968) (R^2 = .468)	Participation (negative impact of role ambiguity)		.362*
			Closeness of supervision (indirect effect)		NS
			Experience (time)		NS
Behrman et al. (1981)	Industrial (n = 193, five companies)	Job satisfaction (Churchill et al. 1974) (R^2 = .47)	Role ambiguity: the expectations of: (Churchill et al. 1974)		(REGR)
			managers		−.35*
			company		.11
			customer		.05
			family		.08

(continued)

Table A-7 (continued)

Situation (Sample Size)	Author (Year)	Criterion Variable (Measurement)	Predictor Variable (Measurement)	(Technique) Strength
Pharmaceutical sales (n = 437, three firms)	Bush & Busch (1981)	Job satisfaction (Smith et al. 1969) pay, work, promotion, supervision, coworkers, customers	Role clarity (Donnelly & Ivancevich 1975)	(CORR) .31* .30* .17* .30* .25* .25*
Retail (n = 203)	Dubinsky & Borys (1981)	Overall job satisfaction (author modified, Donnelly & Ivanovich 1975) (R^2 = .18)	Performance feedback (author scale) Role conflict (author scale) Job experience (number of years) Role ambiguity (author scale)	(REGR) .383* −.140* NS NS
Retail (n = 138)	Teas (1981a)	Satisfaction with work (all author modified, Smith et al. 1969, plus author scales) (R^2 = .497)	Closeness of supervision Task variety Task autonomy Job feedback Participation Company feedback Task significance (All Hackman & Oldham 1975; House & Dessler 1974)	(REGR) .446* .256* .206* .252* NS NS NS
		Satisfaction with supervisor (R^2 = .528)	Closeness of supervision Company feedback Task significance Participation Task variety	.520* .325* .133* NS NS

	Task autonomy	NS
	Job feedback	NS
Satisfaction with pay (R² = .293)	Closeness of supervision	.513*
	Task autonomy	.183*
	Participation	NS
	Company feedback	NS
	Task variety	NS
	Task significance	NS
	Job feedback	NS
Satisfaction with coworkers (R² = .287)	Closeness of supervision	.443*
	Task autonomy	.140*
	Job feedback	.310*
	Participation	NS
	Company feedback	NS
	Task variety	NS
	Task significance	NS
Satisfaction with promotion (R² = .190)	Closeness of supervision	.168*
	Company feedback	.152*
	Task autonomy	.240*
	Participation	NS
	Task variety	NS
	Task significance	NS
	Job feedback	NS
Satisfaction with customers (R² = .184)	Closeness of supervision	.368*
	Task significance	.191*
	Participation	NS
	Company feedback	NS
	Task variety	NS
	Task autonomy	NS
	Job feedback	NS

(continued)

Table A-7 (continued)

Situation (Sample Size)	Author (Year)	Criterion Variable (Measurement)	Predictor Variable (Measurement)	(Technique) Strength
Industrial (n = 188, three companies)	Teas (1981c)	Work satisfaction (Brayfield & Rothe 1974) ($R^2 = .244$)	Skill variety (Hackman & Oldham 1975)	(REGR) .044
			Task identity	−.068
			Task significance	.056
			Autonomy	.243*
			Feedback	.126
			Higher order need strength	−.085
			Variety by higher order need strength	.204*
			Identity by higher order need strength	.048
			Significance by higher order need strength	.151*
			Autonomy by higher order need strength	−.020
			Feedback by higher order need strength	−.040
Industrial products (n = 214)	Becherer et al. (1982)	General satisfaction (Hackman & Oldham 1975 for all variables) ($R^2 = .52$)	Experienced meaningfulness	(REGR) .56*
			Experienced responsibility	.13*
			Knowledge of results	.20*
			Skill variety	−.02
			Task identity	−.07
			Task significance	−.06
			Autonomy	−.03
			Feedback	−.01
		Growth satisfaction ($R^2 = .55$)	Experienced meaningfulness	.48*
			Experienced responsibility	.11*
			Knowledge of results	−.01
			Skill variety	.11
			Task identity	.00

Product/Industry	Author (year)	Dependent variable	Independent variable	Statistic
Industrial distributor (n = 40)	Churchill & Pecotich (1982)	Satisfaction with pay (Churchill et al. 1974; "Faces": Dunham & Herman 1975; Smith et al. 1969; MSQ: Weiss et al. 1967)	Task significance	.00
			Autonomy	.16*
			Feedback	.12*
				(S.E.M.)
		Pay importance	Income (pay) level	−.397*
			Satisfaction with pay	−.497*
Component parts (n = 69)	Franke et al. (1982)	Job satisfaction (Churchill et al. 1974) ($R^2 = .60$)		(REGR)
			Role ambiguity (modified Rizzo et al. 1970)	−.297*
			Role conflict (modified Rizzo et al. 1970)	−.323*
			Internality (modified Rotter 1966)	.240*
			Nights worked	−.200*
Industrial cleaning equipment (n = 89)	Motowidlo (1983)	Voluntary turnover ($R^2 = .091$)		(REGR)
			Withdrawal cognition	(NR)
		Voluntary turnover	Pay amount	NS
			Pay satisfaction	NS
		Withdrawal cognition ($R^2 = .188$)	Pay satisfaction	(NR)
		Withdrawal cognition	Pay amount	NS
Pharmaceutical (n = 216)	Parasuraman & Futrell (1983)	Satisfaction with job (All Churchill et al. 1974)		(CORR)
			Age	NS
			Tenure	NS
			Education	−.136*
			Income	.246*
		Satisfaction with coworkers	Age	NS
			Tenure	NS
			Education	NS
			Income	.185*

(continued)

Table A–7 *(continued)*

Situation (Sample Size)	Author (Year)	Criterion Variable (Measurement)	Predictor Variable (Measurement)	(Technique) Strength
		Satisfaction with supervisor	Age	NS
			Tenure	NS
			Education	NS
			Income	.132*
		Satisfaction with pay	Age	NS
			Tenure	NS
			Education	NS
			Income	.301*
		Satisfaction with promotion and development	Age	−.269*
			Tenure	−.286*
			Education	−.138*
			Income	NS
		Satisfaction with company policies and support	Age	NS
			Tenure	NS
			Education	NS
			Income	.260*
		Satisfaction with customers	Age	.159*
			Tenure	.243*
			Education	NS
			Income	.407*
		Propensity to leave (author scale)	Age	−.244*
			Tenure	−.203*
			Education	.121*
			Income	−.245*
			Satisfaction with job	−.471*
			Satisfaction with coworkers	−.163*
			Satisfaction with supervisor	−.231*
			Satisfaction with pay	−.288*
			Satisfaction with promotion and development	−.205*

Industry (n)	Study	Dependent measure	Independent variable	Statistic
Industrial (n = 116)	Teas (1983)	Job satisfaction (Smith et al. 1969) (R² = .47)	Satisfaction with company policies and support	(REGR) −.407*
			Satisfaction with customers	−.345*
			Consideration	.333*
			Feedback	−.124*
			Participation	.265*
			Experience	.169*
			Role conflict	−.303*
			Initiation of structure	NS
			Role ambiguity	NS
			(All Hackman & Oldham 1975; House & Dessler 1974; Rizzo et al. 1970)	
Retail (n = 121)	Dubinsky & Skinner (1984a)	Overall job satisfaction (Hackman & Oldham 1975) (R² = .48)	Variety	(P.A.) .456*
			Task identity	−.182*
			Role conflict	−.399*
			Role ambiguity	−.192*
			Autonomy	NS
			Feedback	NS
			Performance	NS
			(Rizzo et al. 1970; Sims et al. 1976)	
Retail (n = 157)	Dubinsky & Skinner (1984b)	General job satisfaction (Hackman & Oldham 1975)	Job Status	(ANOVA) Part Time 22.34 — Full Time 22.18 — NS
Retail (n = 157)	Dubinsky & Skinner (1984c)	Overall job satisfaction (Hackman & Oldham 1975)	Age	(CORR) .128
			Job tenure	.109
			Education	−.331*
			Sex	.194*

(continued)

Table A–7 (continued)

Situation (Sample Size)	Author (Year)	Criterion Variable (Measurement)	Predictor Variable (Measurement)	(Technique) Strength
		Organizational commitment (Hrebiniak & Alutto 1972)	Overall job satisfaction	.558*
			Age	.378*
			Job tenure	.318*
			Education	-.427*
			Sex	NS
Industrial equipment (n = 20)	Mahajan et al. (1984)	Total job satisfaction ($R^2 = .39$)	Closeness of supervision	(REGR) 3.23*
		($R^2 = NS$)	Influence over standards	1.20
		($R^2 = .39$)	Role ambiguity	-1.27*
		($R^2 = NS$)	Role conflict	-1.56
		Job itself ($R^2 = .53$)	Closeness of supervision	.63*
		Fellow workers ($R^2 = .27$)	Closeness of supervision	.22*
		Supervision ($R^2 = .33$)	Closeness of supervision	.91*
		Company policies and support ($R^2 = NS$)	Closeness of supervision	.70
		Pay ($R^2 = NS$)	Closeness of supervision	.13
		Promotion and advancement ($R^2 = .25$)	Closeness of supervision	.41*
		Customers ($R^2 = .24$)	Closeness of supervision	.23*
		Job itself ($R^2 = .23$)	Influence over standards	.58*
		Fellow workers ($R^2 = NS$)	Influence over standards	.04
		Supervision ($R^2 = NS$)	Influence over standards	-.10
		Company policies and support ($R^2 = NS$)	Influence over standards	.33
		Pay ($R^2 = NS$)	Influence over standards	.12
		Promotion and advancement ($R^2 = NS$)	Influence over standards	.21
		Customers ($R^2 = NS$)	Influence over standards	.02

Job itself ($R^2 = .47$)	Role ambiguity	$-.23^*$
Fellow workers ($R^2 = .39$)	Role ambiguity	$-.11^*$
Supervision ($R^2 = .30$)	Role ambiguity	$-.34^*$
Company policies and support ($R^2 = .19$)	Role ambiguity	$-.35^*$
Pay ($R^2 = NS$)	Role ambiguity	$-.04$
Promotion and advancement ($R^2 = NS$)	Role ambiguity	$-.08$
Customers ($R^2 = .36$)	Role ambiguity	$-.11^*$
Job itself ($R^2 = NS$)	Role conflict	$.02^*$
Fellow workers ($R^2 = NS$)	Role conflict	$.09$
Supervision ($R^2 = .023$)	Role conflict	$.63^*$
Company policies and support ($R^2 = .23$)	Role conflict	$.70^*$
Pay ($R^2 = NS$)	Role conflict	$-.08$
Promotion and advancement ($R^2 = NS$)	Role conflict	$-.15$
Customers ($R^2 = NS$)	Role conflict	$.05$

Table A–8
Salesperson Job Performance

Situation (Sample Size)	Author (Year)	Criterion Variable (Measurement)	Predictor Variable (Measurement)	(Technique) Strength
Wood products sales (n = 91)	Pruden (1969)	Productivity (Pym & Auld 1965, self rating)	Interorganizational linking (author scale)	(X) Positive relationship
Wood products sales (n = 91)	Pruden & Reese (1972)	Performance (Pym & Auld 1965, self rating) (high vs. low)	Power	(DIS)
			exclusive jurisdiction over customer accounts	—
			influence over credit decisions	—
			influence over delivery time	.176
			influence over type and number of products	—
			influence over pricing	—
			Authority (with regard to):	
			company warehouseman	—
			company inside salesmen	.109
			customer's yardmen	—
			collection of credit	.176
			customer's sales clerks	—
			Status	
			similarity to customers	.102
			familiarity with customers	.128
International Harvester (n = 11, 12)	Darmon (1974)	Performance (sales)	Compensation plan	(S)
			Salary + commission	NS
			Salary + bonus	NS
Life insurance (n = 95)	Oliver (1974)	Sales volume (six-month sales) ($R^2 = .22$)	Valence + instrumentality	(REGR)
			four nonfinancial incentives (membership in three production clubs and invitation to convention)	+ *

	compensation (income)	$(R^2 = NS)$	NS
	intrinsic job outcomes (author scale)	$(R^2 = NS)$	NS
	most desirable job outcomes (subject selected)	$(R^2 = NS)$	NS
	twenty job outcomes	$(R^2 = NS)$	NS
Goal attainment (realized six-month sales volume divided by sales objective)		$R^2 = NS$	
	four nonfinancial incentives	$(R^2 = NS)$	NS
	compensation	$(R^2 = NS)$	NS
	intrinsic job outcomes	$(R^2 = NS)$	NS
	twenty job outcomes	$(R^2 = NS)$	NS
			(CORR)
Sales volume	Aggregate valence		
	four nonfinancial		.433*
	compensation		.036
	intrinsic		−.150
	most desirable job outcomes		—
	twenty job outcomes		.043
Goal attainment	four nonfinancial incentives		.238*
	compensation		.068
	intrinsic job outcomes		−.070
	most desirable job outcomes		—
	twenty job outcomes		−.018
Sales volume	Aggregate instrumentality		
	four nonfinancial incentives		.429*
	compensation		.225*
	intrinsic job outcomes		.093
	most desirable job outcomes		.153
	twenty job outcomes		−.168

(continued)

Table A–8 *(continued)*

Situation (Sample Size)	Author (Year)	Criterion Variable (Measurement)	Predictor Variable (Measurement)	(Technique) Strength
		Goal attainment	four nonfinancial incentives	.148*
			compensation	.112
			intrinsic job outcomes	.070
			most desirable job outcomes	.090
			twenty job outcomes	.070
		Sales volume	Aggregate valence × instrumentality	
			four nonfinancial incentives	.480*
			compensation	.022
			intrinsic job outcomes	−.105
			most desirable job outcomes	.172
			twenty job outcomes	.112
		Goal attainment	four nonfinancial incentives	.201*
			compensation	.055
			intrinsic job outcomes	−.032
			most desirable job outcomes	.102
			twenty job outcomes	.048
				(REGR)
		Sales volume	Valence + performance expectancy	
		(R^2 = .248)	four nonfinancial incentives	+*
		(R^2 = NS)	compensation	NS
		(R^2 = .084)	intrinsic job outcomes	+*
		(R^2 = .084)	most desirable job outcomes	+*
		(R^2 = NS)	twenty job outcomes	NS
		Goal attainment	four nonfinancial incentives	+*
		(R^2 = .109)	compensation	+*
		(R^2 = .096)	intrinsic job outcomes	+*
		(R^2 = .099)	most desirable job outcomes	+*
		(R^2 = .097)	twenty job outcomes	+*
		(R^2 = .096)		

Study	Dependent variable	Independent/moderator variable	Result
	Goal attainment	four nonfinancial incentives	(CORR) .259*
		compensation	.171
		intrinsic job outcomes	.060
		most desirable job outcomes	.245*
		twenty job outcomes	.135
	Sales volume	four nonfinancial incentives	.502*
		compensation	.131
		intrinsic job outcomes	−.025
		most desirable job outcomes	.269*
		twenty job outcomes	.174
Ivancevich & Donnelly (1975)	Performance: absenteeism (number times absent from job)	Organizational structure (Berry & Sadler 1967)	(ANOVA)
Consumer trade sales to retail store (n = 295)		tall	NS
		medium	NS
		flat	NS
	Efficiency rating (total number of orders divided by total retail outlets visited)	tall	.22*
		medium	.28*
		flat	.48*
	Route coverage (miles traveled divided by number retail outlets visited)	tall	NS
		medium	NS
		flat	NS
Futrell et al. (1976)	Performance (author/firm supervisor rating form of sales reps on ten dimensions)	Clarity variable	(CTA)
Pharmaceutical (n = 431, two firms)		unclear on superior's opinion	.03*
		clear on results expected	.02*
	Improvement in total job performance over previous year	clear on relative importance of goals	NS

(continued)

Table A–8 (continued)

Situation (Sample Size)	Author (Year)	Criterion Variable (Measurement)	Predictor Variable (Measurement)	(Technique) Strength
			Influence and control variable	
			control over means of doing job	NS
			have little control and final say	NS
			influence in setting job goals	NS
			allowed to be creative	NS
			challenged by work	NS
			no need to develop new job ideas	NS
			Performance-reward variable	.04*
			reward follows performance	
			have incentive to do better	.01*
			relative well rewarded financially	.02*
			best men promoted	
		Current product knowledge	Clarity	
			unclear on superior's opinion	.03*
			all other variables	NS
		Current human relations ability	Clarity	
			clear on relative importance of goals	.04*
			All other variables	NS
		Current sales ability	Clarity	
			unclear on superior's opinion	.009*
			Influence and control	
			have little control and final say	.008*
			All other variables	NS
		Current overall job performance	Clarity	
			unclear on superior's opinion	.009*
			All other variables	NS

Category	Variable	Significance
	Influence and control	
	have little control and final say	.03
	All other variables	NS
Current general attitude	Clarity	
	unclear on superior's opinion	.004*
	clear on results expected	.002*
	clear on relative importance of goals	.02*
	Influence and control	
	control over means of doing job	NS
	have little control and final say	.000
	influence in setting job goals	.006
	allowed to be creative	NS
	challenged by work	.002
	no need to develop new job ideas	.008
	Performance rewards	
	reward follows performance	.000*
	have incentive to do better	.000*
	relatively well rewarded financially	.000*
	best men promoted	.008*
Willingness to work hard	Clarity	
	unclear on superior's opinion	.000*
	clear on results expected	.000*
	clear on relative importance of goals	.009*
	Influence and control	
	control over means of doing job	NS
	have little control and final say	.000*
	influence in setting job goals	.025*
	allowed to be creative	NS
	challenged by work	.01*
	no need to develop new job ideas	NS
	Performance reward	
	reward follows performance	.004*
	have incentive to do better	.000*

(continued)

Table A–8 (continued)

Situation (Sample Size)	Author (Year)	Criterion Variable (Measurement)	Predictor Variable (Measurement)	(Technique) Strength
		Planning ability	relatively well rewarded financially	.000*
			best men promoted	.01*
			Clarity	
			unclear on superior's opinion	.03*
			Influence and control	
			challenged by work	.03*
			All other variables	NS
		Coverage of territory	Influence and control	.02*
			All other variables	NS
		Activity reporting	Clarity	
			unclear on superior's opinion	.02*
			clear on results expected	.05*
			All other variables	NS
Hospital products (n = 67)	Futrell et al. (1977)		Management by Objectives Program	(Z)
				Before program/ After program
		Performance improvement		7.33*
		Product knowledge		3.66*
		Human relations		2.78*
		Sales ability		3.81*
		Current performance		4.26*
		Work hard		4.40*
		Planning ability		4.88*
		Territory coverage		NS
		Activity reporting		NS
		Attitude		4.25*
				(Results were higher after the MBO program than before the MBO program)

Sample	Study	Performance measure	Variables		Statistic
Industrial (n = 107)	Small & Rosenberg (1977)	Performance (3-year sales average) ($R^2 = .47$)	Life history variables age marital status experience interviewer's evaluation sales aptitude education salary record		(REGR) (NR)
		Performance (3-year sales average) ($R^2 = .36$)	Personality variables ascendancy cautiousness emotional stability original thinking personal relations responsibility sociability vigor		(NR)
		Performance (3-year sales average) ($R^2 = .81$)	Combined list of life history and personality variables		(NR)
Steel strapping (n = 160)	Bagozzi (1978)	Performance (annual sales) ($R^2 = .40$)	Territory potential (industry sales) Job tension (Kahn 1964) Verbal intelligence (Borgatta 1971) Specific self esteem (author scale) Generalized self esteem (Jackson 1975) Role ambiguity (Ford et al. 1975) Territory workload (number of accounts) Other-directedness (Collins et al. 1973)		(REGR) .151* −9.2* −12.6* 9.3* NS NS NS NS
Pharmaceutical (n = 477)	Busch & Bush (1978)	Performance (self rating: Pruden & Reese 1972)	Role Clarity (Donnelly & Ivancevich 1975) Males Females		(CORR) .52* .21

Table A–8 (continued)

Situation (Sample Size)	Author (Year)	Criterion Variable (Measurement)	Predictor Variable (Measurement)	(Technique) Strength
Pharmaceutical (n = 508)	Futrell & Jenkins (1978)	Performance (supervisor rating) product knowledge activity reporting human relations ability coverage of territory overall job performance	Pay disclosure vs. secrecy (in the direction of pay disclosure)	(ANOVA) + * + * + * + * + * + *
Pharmaceutical (n = 431, two companies)	Swan & Futrell (1978)	Performance improvement product knowledge sales ability overall performance territory coverage activity reporting human relations attitude work hard planning	Sex	(X) + + + + + NS + + + (Sign in direction of males)
Steel strapping (n = 122)	Aaker & Bagozzi (1979)	Performance (annual sales 1 year)	Job tension Self esteem	(S.E.M.) −.23* .60*
Retail (n = 203)	Dubinsky & Mattson (1979)	Performance (Pruden & Reese 1972, self rating)	Role conflict Role ambiguity (author scales)	(CORR) −.21* −.25*
Steel strapping (n = 122)	Bagozzi (1980a)	Performance (annual dollar sales)	Task-specific self esteem (author scale)	(C.M.L) .959*

Sample	Author	Performance measure	Variable	Result
Steel strapping (n = 122)	Bagozzi (1980b)	Performance (annual sales)	Verbal intelligence (Borgatta 1971)	−.179*
			Job satisfaction (author scale)	.258*
				(REGR)
			Role ambiguity (Duncan 1969)	−.348*
			Motivation (Kahn et al. 1964)	.380*
Industrial chemicals (n = 148)	Berkowitz (1980)	Self-rated performance		(CORR)
			Role clarity (author scale)	.28*
			Role strain (author scale)	−.20*
		Performance measures		
		personal sales volume	Role clarity/strain	−.02/−.02
		district net profit	Role clarity/strain	NS
		district turnover	Role clarity/strain	NS
		district sales to expense	Role clarity/strain	NS
Retail (n = 203)	Dubinsky & Mattson (1980)	Performance (self rated; Pruden & Reese 1972)	Sex	Male Female
				NS
Industrial products (n = 200, five firms)	Behrman et al. (1981)	Performance (author scale, supervisor rating)	Locus of control (Rotter 1966)	(MANOVA) Medium (+) better; Low (internal); High (external)
			Need for clarity (Lyons 1971)	Low need (+) better than medium or high need
		Performance (same measure) (R² = .25)	Role ambiguity (Churchill et al. 1974)	(REGR)
			Expectations of:	
			manager	−.19*
			company	NS
			customer	−.16*
			family	.17*

(continued)

Table A-8 (continued)

Situation (Sample Size)	Author (Year)	Criterion Variable (Measurement)	Predictor Variable (Measurement)	(Technique) Strength
Pharmaceutical (n = 437)	Bush & Busch (1981)	Performance (Pym & Auld 1965, self rating)	Role clarity (Donnelly & Ivancevich 1975)	(CORR) .14*
Retail (n = 203)	Dubinsky & Borys (1981)	Performance (modified Pruden & Reese 1972, self rating)	Role ambiguity (author scale)	−.313*
			Role conflict (author scale)	NS
			Job experience (number of years)	NS
			Performance feedback (author scale)	NS
Industrial sales to O.E.M. (n = 69)	Franke et al. (1982)	Performance (Behrman & Perreault 1982, self rating) ($R^2 = .34$)	Role ambiguity (modified Rizzo et al. 1970)	(REGR) −.421*
			Experience (numbers of years selling)	.321*
			Role conflict (modified Rizzo et al. 1970)	NS
Industrial (n = 63)	Cravens et al. (1983)	Sales (dollars) ($R^2 = .26$)	Pay	(REGR) Significant, NR
			Sex	Significant, NR
			Market potential	Significant, NR
			Market share	Significant, NR
			Workload	NS
			Tenure	NS
			Age	NS
		Percent of sales quota ($R^2 = .21$)	Market potential	Significant, NR
			Market share	Significant, NR
			Workload	NS
			Pay	NS
			Sex	NS
			Tenure	NS
			Age	NS

Sample	Study	Performance measure	Predictor	Result
Pharmaceutical (n = 399)	Futrell et al. (1983)	Performance (manager rated)	Effort (author scale)	(CORR) .135*
Real estate agents and brokers (n = 70)	Rafaeli & Klimoski (1983)	Number of sales Number of listings Dollar amount of sales Dollar amount of commission Global index of performance	Handwriting samples (neutral description versus autobiographical description)	(CORR) Both NS
Retail (n = 116)	Dubinsky & Skinner (1984a)	Performance (year-to-date sales) ($R^2 = .07$)	Autonomy Role ambiguity Variety Task identity Feedback Role conflict Work motivation (Hackman & Oldham 1975; Rizzo et al. 1970)	(P.A.) .173* -.157* NS NS NS NS NS
Retail (n = 157)	Dubinsky & Skinner (1984b)	Performance (Pruden & Reese 1972, self rating)	Job status	(ANOVA) Part Time Full Time 2.88 3.16*

References

Aaker, A. and R.P. Bagozzi (1979), "Unobservable Variables in Structural Equation Models with an Application in Industrial Selling," *Journal of Marketing Research,* 16 (May), 147–158.

The Art and Science of Selling (1918), Vol. 1: *The Salesman* (Chicago: National Salesmen's Training Association).

Austin, R.L. (1954), "The Selection of Sales Personnel: A Review of Research," unpublished Ed.D. thesis, Graduate School of Business, Indiana University.

Baehr, M.E. and G.B. Williams (1967), "Underlying Dimensions of Personal Background Data and Their Relationship to Occupational Classification," *Journal of Applied Psychology,* 51 (December), 481–490.

Baehr, M.E. and G.B. Williams (1968), "Prediction of Sales Success from Factorially Determined Dimensions of Personal Background Data," *Journal of Applied Psychology,* 52 (April), 98–103.

Bagozzi, R.P. (1978), "Salesforce Performance and Satisfaction as a Function of Individual Difference, Interpersonal, and Situational Factors," *Journal of Marketing Research,* 15 (November), 517–531.

Bagozzi, R.P. (1980a), "Performance and Satisfaction in an Industrial Sales Force: An Examination of Their Antecedents and Simultaneity," *Journal of Marketing,* 44 (Spring), 65–77.

Bagozzi, R.P. (1980b), "The Nature and Causes of Self-Esteem, Performance, and Satisfaction in the Sales Force: A Structural Equation Approach," *Journal of Business,* 53 (July), 315–331.

Baier, D. and R.D. Dugan (1957), "Factors in Sales Success," *Journal of Applied Psychology,* 41 (February), 37–40.

Becherer, R.C., F.W. Morgan, and L.M. Richard (1982), "The Job Characteristics of Industrial Salespersons: Relationship to Motivation and Satisfaction," *Journal of Marketing,* 46 (October), 125–135.

Behrman, D.N., W.J. Bigoness, and W.D. Perrault (1981), "Job Related Ambiguity and Its Consequences Upon Salespersons' Job Satisfaction," *Management Science,* 11 (November), 1246–1260.

Behrman, D.N. and W.D. Perreault (1982), "Measuring the Performance of Industrial Salespersons," *Journal of Business Research,* 10 (September), 355–370.

Belasco, J.A. (1966), "The Salesman's Role Revisited," *Journal of Marketing,* 30 (April), 6–9.

Berkowitz, E.N. (1980), "Role Theory, Attitudinal Constructs, and Actual Performance: A Measurement Issue," *Journal of Applied Psychology,* 65 (April), 240–245.

Berry, B.A. and P.J. Sadler (1967), "Organizational Characteristics of Growing Companies," *Journal of Management Studies,* 4, 204–219.

Berry, L. (1969), "The Components of Department Store Image: A Theoretical and Empirical Analysis," *Journal of Retailing,* 45 (Spring), 3–20.

Borgatta, E.F. (1971), "Intelligent Word Associations," *Multivariate Behavioral Research,* 6 (July), 301–311.

Brayfield, A.H. and H.F. Rothe (1974), "Job Satisfaction Index," in *Measures of Occupational Attitudes and Occupational Characteristics,* J.P. Robinson, R. Anathasiou, and B.H. Kendra, eds. (Ann Arbor, MI: Institute for Social Research, University of Michigan).

Brown, S.H. (1978), "Long-Term Validity of a Personnel History Item Scoring Procedure," *Journal of Applied Psychology,* 63 (December), 673–676.

Burke, R.J. and D.S. Wilcox (1971), "Bases of Supervisory Power and Subordinate Job Satisfactions," *Canadian Journal of Behavioral Science,* 3 (April), 183–193.

Burstiner, I. (1975–1976), "Current Personnel Practices in Department Stores," *Journal of Retailing,* 51 (Winter), 3–14ff.

Busch, P. (1980), "The Sales Manager's Bases of Social Power and Influence Upon the Sales Force," *Journal of Marketing,* 44 (Summer), 91–101.

Busch, P. and R.F. Bush (1978), "Women Contrasted to Men in the Industrial Sales Force: Job Satisfaction, Values, Role Clarity, Performance, and Propensity to Leave," *Journal of Marketing Research,* 15 (August), 438–448.

Bush, R.F. and P. Busch (1979), "The Relationship of Tenure and Age to Job Satisfaction in the Industrial Sales Force," in 1979 AMA Educators' Conference *Proceedings,* N. Beckwith et al., eds. (Chicago: American Marketing Association), 417–421.

Bush, R.F. and P. Busch (1981), "The Relationship of Tenure and Age to Role Clarity and Its Consequences in the Industrial Sales Force," *Journal of Personal Selling and Sales Management,* 2 (Fall/Winter), 17–23.

Campbell, J.P. and R.D. Pritchard (1976), "Motivation Theory in Industrial and Organizational Psychology," in *Handbook of Industrial and Organizational Psychology,* M.D. Dunnette, ed. (Chicago: Rand McNally), 63–130.

Chonko, L.B. (1982), "The Relationship of Span of Control to Sales Representatives' Experienced Role Conflict and Role Ambiguity," *Academy of Management Journal,* 25 (June), 452–456.

Churchill, G.A., N.M. Ford, O.C. Walker (1974), "Measuring the Job Satisfaction of Industrial Salesmen," *Journal of Marketing Research,* 11 (August), 254–260.

Churchill, G.A., R.H. Collins, and W.A. Strang (1975), "Should Retail Salespersons Be Similar to Their Customers?" *Journal of Retailing,* 51 (Fall), 29–42.

Churchill, G.A., N.M. Ford, and O.C. Walker (1976), "Organizational Climate and Job Satisfaction in the Sales Force," *Journal of Marketing Research,* 13 (November), 323–332.

Churchill, G.A., N.M. Ford, and O.C. Walker (1979), "Personal Characteristics of Salespeople and Attractiveness of Alternative Rewards," *Journal of Business Research,* 7 (Number 1), 25–50.

Churchill, G.A., N.M. Ford, and O.C. Walker (1981), *Sales Force Management* (Homewood, IL: Richard D. Irwin).

Churchill, G.A., and A. Pecotich (1982), "A Structural Equation Investigation of the Pay Satisfaction-Valence Relationship Among Salespeople," *Journal of Marketing,* 46 (Fall), 114–124.

Claxton, J.D. and J.R.B. Ritchie (1979), "Consumer Prepurchase Shopping Problems: A Focus on the Retail Component," *Journal of Retailing,* 55 (Fall), 24–43.

Collins, B.E., J.C. Martin, R.D. Ashmore, and L. Ross (1973), "Some Dimensions of the Internal-External Metaphors in Theories of Personality," *Journal of Personality,* 41 (December), 471–492.

Connolly, T. (1976), "Some Conceptual and Methodological Issues in Expectancy Models of Work Performance Motivation," *Academy of Management Review,* 1 (October), 34–47.

Cotham, J.C. III (1968), "Job Attitudes and Sales Performance of Major Appliance Salesmen," *Journal of Marketing Research,* 5 (November), 370–375.

Cotham, J.C. III (1969), "Using Personal History Information in Retail Salesman Selection," *Journal of Retailing,* 45 (Summer), 31–38ff.

Cravens, D.W., D.W. Finn, and W.C. Moncrief (1983), "Relationship of Uncontrollable Sales Territory Variables to Salesperson Performance," in 1983 AMA Educators' Conference *Proceedings,* P.E. Murphy et al., eds. (Chicago: American Marketing Association), 198–202.

Crissy, W.J.E., P.M. Fischer, and F.H. Mossman (1973), "Segmental Analysis: Key to Marketing Profitability," *MSU Business Topics,* 21 (Spring), 42–49.

Darmon, R.Y. (1974), "Salesmen's Response to Financial Incentives: An Empirical Study," *Journal of Marketing Research,* 11 (November), 418–426.

Darmon, R.Y. (1979), "Setting Sales Quotas with Conjoint Analysis," *Journal of Marketing Research,* 16 (February), 133–140.

Day, R.L. and P.D. Bennett (1962), "Should Salesmen's Compensation be Geared to Profits?" *Journal of Marketing,* 26 (October), 6–9.

Dillard, J.F. (1981), "So, Where Do We Go From Here?" *Decision Sciences,* 12 (January), 46–50.

Donnelly, J.H. and J.M. Ivancevich (1975), "Role Clarity and the Salesman," *Journal of Marketing,* 39 (January), 71–74.

Doyle, S.X. and B.P. Shapiro (1980), "What Counts Most in Motivating Your Sales Force?" *Harvard Business Review,* 58 (May–June), 133–140.

Dubin, R. (1958), *The World of Work* (Englewood Cliffs, NJ: Prentice-Hall).

Dubinsky, A.J. and B.E. Mattson (1979), "Consequences of Role Conflict and Ambiguity Experienced by Retail Salespeople," *Journal of Retailing,* 55 (Winter), 70–86.

Dubinsky, A.J. and B.E. Mattson (1980), "Differences Between Male and Female Retail Salespeople's Job Satisfaction, Performance, Organizational Commitment, Role Conflict, and Role Ambiguity," in 1980 AMA Educators' Conference *Proceedings,* R.P. Bagozzi et al., eds. (Chicago: American Marketing Association), 229–233.

Dubinsky, A.J. and R.H. Borys (1981), "A Path Analytic Study of Causes and Consequences of Retail Salespeople's Role Conflict and Ambiguity," in 1981 AMA Educators' Conference *Proceedings,* K. Bernhardt et al., eds. (Chicago: American Marketing Association), 35–38.

Dubinsky, A.J. and T.E. Barry (1982), "A Survey of Sales Management Practices," *Industrial Marketing Management,* 11 (April), 133–142.

Dubinsky, A.J. and S.J. Skinner (1984a), "Impact of Job Characteristics on Retail

Salespeople's Reaction to Their Jobs," *Journal of Retailing,* 60 (Summer), 35–63.

Dubinsky, A.J. and S.J. Skinner (1984b), "Job Status and Employees' Responses: Effects of Demographic Characteristics," *Psychological Reports,* 55 (Summer), 323–328.

Dubinsky, A.J. and S.J. Skinner (1984c), "Turnover Tendencies Among Retail Salespeople: Relationships with Job Satisfaction and Demographic Variables," in 1984 AMA Educators' Conference *Proceedings,* R.W. Belk et al., eds. (Chicago: American Marketing Association), 153–157.

Duncan, O.D. (1969), "Contingencies in Constructing Causal Models," in *Sociological Methodology,* E.F. Borgatta, ed. (San Francisco, CA: Jossey-Bass, Inc.)

Dunham, R.B. and J.B. Herman (1975), "Development of Female Faces Scale for Measuring Job Satisfaction," *Journal of Applied Psychology,* 60 (October), 629–631.

Dunnette, M.D. and W.K. Kirchner (1960), "Psychological Test Differences Between Industrial Salesmen and Retail Salesmen," *Journal of Applied Psychology,* 45 (April), 121–125.

Einhorn, H.J. (1971), "Use of Nonlinear, Noncompensatory Models as a Function of Task and Amount of Information," *Organizational Behavior and Human Performance,* 6 (January), 1–27.

Evans, F.B. (1963), "Selling as a Dyadic Relationship: A New Approach," *The American Behavioral Scientist,* 6 (May), 76–79.

Farley, J.U. (1964), "Optimal Plan for Salesmen's Compensation," *Journal of Marketing Research,* 1 (May), 39–43.

Ford, N.M., O.C. Walker, and G.A. Churchill (1975), "Expectation—Specific Measures of the Intersender Conflict and Role Ambiguity Experienced by Industrial Salesmen," *Journal of Business Research,* 3 (April), 95–111.

Franke, G.R., D.N. Behrman, and W.D. Perreault (1982), "Sales Force Performance and Satisfaction: Contemporaneous Relationships and Selected Antecedents," in 1982 AMA Educators' Conference *Proceedings,* B.J. Walker et al., eds. (Chicago: American Marketing Association), 233–237.

French, C.L. (1960), "Correlates of Success in Retail Selling," *American Journal of Sociology,* 66 (September), 128–134.

Futrell, C.M. (1979), "Sales Force Job Attitudes, Design, and Behavior," *Journal of the Academy of Marketing Science,* 7 (Spring), 101–107.

Futrell, C.M., J.E. Swan, and J.T. Todd (1976), "Job Performance Related to Management Control Systems for Pharmaceutical Salesmen," *Journal of Marketing Research,* 13 (February), 25–33.

Futrell, C.M., J.E. Swan, and C.W. Lamb (1977), "Benefits and Problems in a Sales Force MBO System," *Industrial Marketing Management,* 6, 265–272.

Futrell, C.M. and O.C. Jenkins (1978), "Pay Secrecy Versus Pay Disclosure for Salesmen: A Longitudinal Study," *Journal of Marketing Research,* 16 (May), 214–219.

Futrell, C.M., A. Parasuraman, and J. Sager (1983), "Sales Force Evaluation with Expectancy Theory," *Industrial Marketing Management,* 12 (April), 125–129.

Ghiselli, E.E. (1969), "Prediction of Success of Stockbrokers," *Personnel Psychology,* 22 (Summer), 125–130.

Ghiselli, E.E. (1973), "The Validity of Aptitude Tests in Personnel Selection," *Personnel Psychology,* 26 (Winter), 461–477.

Graen, G. (1969), "Instrumentality Theory of Work Motivation: Some Experimental Results and Suggested Modifications," *Journal of Applied Psychology,* 53 (April), 1–25.

Greenberg, H. and D. Mayer (1964), "A New Approach to the Scientific Selection of Successful Salesmen," *Journal of Psychology,* 57 (January), 113–123.

Hackman, J.R. and G.K. Oldham (1975), "The Development of the Job Diagnostic Survey," *Journal of Applied Psychology,* 60 (April), 159–170.

Halpin, A.W. and B.J. Winer (1957), "A Factorial Study of Leader Behavior Description," in *Leader Behavior: Its Description and Measurement,* A.M. Stogdill and A.E. Coons, eds. (Columbus, OH: Bureau of Business Research).

Hansen, R.A. and T. Deutscher (1977–1978), "An Empirical Investigation of Attribute Importance in Retail Store Selection," *Journal of Retailing,* 53 (Winter), 59–72.

Harrell, T.W. (1960), "The Relation of Test Scores to Sales Criteria," *Personnel Psychology,* 13 (Spring), 65–69.

Hise, R.T. (1970), "Conflict in the Salesman's Role," in *Sales Management: Contemporary Perspectives,* J.A. Barnhill, ed. (Glenview, IL: Scott, Foresman), 48–62.

House, R.J. and G. Dessler (1974), "The Path-Goal Theory of Leadership: Some Post Hoc and A Priori Tests," in *Contingency Approaches to Leadership,* J.G. Hunt and L.L. Larson, eds. (Carbondale, IL: Southern Illinois University Press).

Howells, G.W. (1968), "The Successful Salesman: A Personality Analysis," *British Journal of Marketing,* 2, 13–23.

Hrebiniak, L.G. and J.A. Alutto (1972), "Personal and Role-Related Factors in the Development of Organizational Commitment," *Administrative Science Quarterly,* 17 (December), 555–573.

Indik, B., S.E. Seashore, and J. Slesinger (1964), "Demographic Correlates of Psychological Strain," *Journal of Abnormal and Social Psychology,* 69 (July), 26–38.

Ingram, T.N. and D.N. Bellenger (1983), "Personal and Organizational Variables: Their Relative Effect on Reward Valences of Industrial Salespeople," *Journal of Marketing Research,* 20 (May), 198–205.

Ivancevich, J.M. and J.H. Donnelly (1975), "Relation of Organizational Structure to Job Satisfaction, Anxiety-Stress, and Performance," *Administrative Science Quarterly,* 20 (June), 272–279.

Jackson, D. (1975), "The Jackson Personality Inventory," in *Measures of Social Psychological Research* (Ann Arbor, MI: Survey Center Institute for Social Research, University of Michigan).

Jackson, D.W., J.E. Keith, and J.L. Schlachter (1983), "Evaluation of Selling Performance: A Study of Current Practices," *Journal of Personal Selling and Sales Management,* 3 (November), 42–51.

Jolson, M.A. and W.F. Spath (1973), "Understanding and Fulfilling Shoppers' Requirements: An Anomaly in Retailing?" *Journal of Retailing,* 49 (Summer), 38–46.

Jones, A.P. and L.R. James (1977), "Psychology and Organizational Climate: Dimensions and Relationships," Tech. Reg. 76-4 (Fort Worth, TX: Texas Christian University, Institute of Behavioral Research).

Kahn, R.L., D.M. Wolfe, R.P. Quinn, J.D. Snoek, and R.A. Rosenthal (1964), *Organizational Stress: Studies in Role Conflict and Ambiguity,* New York: John Wiley and Sons, Inc.).

Kerr, W.A. and B.J. Speroff (1951), *The Empathy Test* (Chicago: Psychometric Affiliates).

Kirchner, W., C.S. McElwain, and M.D. Dunnette (1960), "A Note on the Relationship between Age and Sales Effectiveness," *Journal of Applied Psychology,* 44 (April), 92–93.

Kirpalani, V.H. and S.S. Shapiro (1973), "Financial Dimensions of Marketing Management," *Journal of Marketing,* 37 (July), 40–47.

Lamont, L.M. and W.J. Lundstrom (1977), "Identifying Successful Industrial Salesmen by Personality and Personal Characteristics," *Journal of Marketing Research,* 14 (November), 517–529.

Lawler, E.E. (1973), *Motivation in Work Organizations,* (Monterey, CA: Brooks/ Cole).

Levinson, T. (1975), "Role, Personality, and Social Structure," in *Sociological Theory: A Book of Readings,* L.A. Coser and B. Rosenberg, eds. (New York: Macmillan), 251–263.

Lodahl, T.M. and M. Kejner (1965), "The Definition and Measurement of Job Involvement," *Journal of Applied Psychology,* 49 (February), 24–33.

Lyons, T.F. (1971), "Role Clarity, Need for Clarity, Satisfaction, Tension, and Withdrawal," *Organizational Behavior and Human Performance,* 6 (January), 99–110.

Mahajan, J., G.A. Churchill, N.M. Ford, and O.C. Walker (1984), "A Comparison of the Impact of Organizational Climate on the Job Satisfaction of Manufacturers' Agents and Company Salespeople: An Exploratory Study," *Journal of Personal Selling and Sales Management,* 4 (May), 1–11.

Matsui, T., M. Kagawa, J. Nagamatsu, and Y. Ohtsuka (1977), "Validity of Expectancy Theory as a Within Person Behavioral Choice Model for Sales Activities," *Journal of Applied Psychology,* 63 (December), 764–767.

Mattheiss, T.H., R.M. Durand, J.R. Muczyk, and M. Gable (1974), "Personality and the Prediction of Salesmen's Success," in *New Marketing for Social and Economics Progress,* R.C. Curhan, ed. (Chicago: American Marketing Association), 499–502.

Mayer, D. and H. Greenberg (1964), "What Makes A Good Salesman?" *Harvard Business Review,* 42 (July–August), 119–125.

McCarthy, E.J. (1981), *Basic Marketing* (Homewood, IL: Richard D. Irwin, Inc.).

Merenda, P.F. and W.V. Clarke (1959), "Predictive Efficiency of Temperament Characteristics and Personal History Variables in Determining Success of Life Insurance Agents," *Journal of Applied Psychology,* 43 (December), 360–366.

Miner, J.B. (1962), "Personality and Ability Factors in Sales Performance," *Journal of Applied Psychology,* 46 (February), 6–13.

Mosel, J.N. (1952), "Prediction of Department Store Sales Performance from Personnel Data," *Journal of Applied Psychology,* 36 (February), 8–10.

Motowidlo, S.J. (1983), "Predicting Sales Turnover from Pay Satisfaction and Expectation," *Journal of Applied Psychology,* 68 (August), 484–489.

Oliver, R.L. (1974), "Expectancy Theory Predictions of Salesmen's Performance," *Journal of Marketing Research,* 11 (August), 243–253.

Oliver, R.L. (1977), "Antecedents of Salesmen's Compensation Perceptions: A Path Analysis Interpretation," *Journal of Applied Psychology,* 62 (February), 20–28.

Oliver, R.L. (1978), "Alternative Conceptions of the Motivation Components in

Expectancy Theory," in *Proceedings from AMA/MSI Workshop,* R. Bagozzi, ed. (Cambridge, MA: American Marketing Association/Marketing Science Institute), 40–63.

Parasuraman, A. and C.M. Futrell (1983), "Demographics, Job Satisfaction, and Propensity to Leave of Industrial Salesmen," *Journal of Business Research,* 11 (March), 33–48.

Parsons, T. (1951), *The Social System* (Glencoe, IL: The Free Press).

Payne, Roy (1976), "Organizational Structure and Climate," in *Handbook of Industrial and Organizational Psychology,* M.D. Dunnette, ed. (Chicago: Rand McNally and Co.), 1125–1174.

Perreault, W.D., W.A. French, and C.E. Harris (1977), "Use of Multiple Discriminant Analysis to Improve the Salesman Selection Process," *Journal of Business,* 50 (January), 50–63.

Perreault, W.D. and R.H. Miles (1978), "Influence Strategy Mixes in Complex Organizations," *Behavioral Science,* 23 (March), 86–98.

Porter, L.W. (1961), "A Study of Perceived Need Satisfactions in Bottom and Middle Management Jobs," *Journal of Applied Psychology,* 45 (February), 1–10.

Porter, L.W. and E.E. Lawler (1968), *Managerial Attitudes and Performance,* (Homewood, IL: The Dorsey Press).

Pruden, H.O. (1969), "Interorganizational Conflict, Linkage, and Exchange: A Study of Industrial Salesmen," *Academy of Management Journal,* 12 (September), 339–350.

Pruden, H.O. and R.A. Peterson (1971), "Personality and Performance-Satisfaction of Industrial Salesmen," *Journal of Marketing Research,* 8 (November), 501–504.

Pruden, H.O., W.H. Cunningham, and W.D. English (1972), "Nonfinancial Incentives for Salesmen," *Journal of Marketing,* 36 (October), 55–59.

Pruden, H.O. and R.M. Reese (1972), "Interorganizational Role-Set Relations and the Performance and Satisfaction of Industrial Salesmen," *Administrative Science Quarterly,* 17 (December), 601–609.

Pym, D.S.A. and H.D. Auld (1965), "The Self-Rating as a Measure of Employee Satisfaction," *Occupational Psychology,* 39, 103–113.

Rafaeli, A. and R.J. Klimoski (1983), "Predicting Sales Success through Handwriting Analysis: An Evaluation of the Effects of Training and Handwriting Sample Content," *Journal of Applied Psychology,* 68 (May), 212–217.

Rizzo, J.R., R.J. House, and S.I. Lirtzman (1970), "Role Conflict and Ambiguity in Complex Organizations," *Administrative Science Quarterly,* 15 (June), 150–163.

Rotter, J.B. (1966), "Generalized Expectancies for Internal vs. External Control of Reinforcement," *Psychological Monographs,* 80 (No. 1).

Scheibelhut, J.H. and G. Albaum (1973), "Self-Other Orientations Among Salesmen and Non-Salesmen," *Journal of Marketing Research,* 10 (February), 97–99.

Schmidt, F.L. (1973), "Implications of a Measurement Problem for Expectancy Theory Research," *Organizational Behavior and Human Performance,* 10 (October), 243–251.

Schwab, D.P., J.D. Gottlieb, and H.G. Heneman (1979), "Between-Subjects Expectancy Theory Research: A Statistical Review of Studies Predicting Effort and Performance," *Psychological Bulletin,* 86 (January), 139–147.

Simon, H.A. (1956), *Models of Man* (New York: John Wiley).

Sims, H.P., A.P. Szilagyi, and R.T. Keller (1976), "The Measurement of Job Characteristics," *Academy of Management Journal,* 19 (June), 195–212.

Small, R.J. and L.J. Rosenberg (1977), "Determining Job Performance in the Industrial Sales Force," *Industrial Marketing Management,* 6 (Number 2), 99–102.

Smith, P.C., L.M. Kendall, and C.L. Hulin (1969), *The Measurement of Satisfaction in Work and Retirement* (Chicago: Rand McNally).

Spivey, W.A., J.M. Munson, and W.B. Locander (1979), "Meeting Retail Staffing Needs via Improved Selection," *Journal of Retailing,* 55 (Winter), 3–19.

Steers, R.M. (1981), *Introduction to Organizational Behavior* (Santa Monica: Goodyear).

Steinbrink, J.P. (1978), "How to Pay Your Sales Force," *Harvard Business Review,* 56 (July–August), 111–122.

Steps into Sales (1981) (Hartford, CN: Life Insurance Marketing and Research Association).

Swan, J.E. and C.M. Futrell (1978), "Men versus Women in Industrial Sales: A Performance Gap," *Industrial Marketing Management,* 7 (December), 369–373.

Tanofsky, R.R., R. Shepps, and P.J. O'Neill (1969), "Pattern Analysis of Biographical Predictors of Success as an Insurance Salesman," *Journal of Applied Psychology,* 53 (April), 136–139.

Tansky, C. (1963), *Career Anchorage Points of Middle Managers,* unpublished doctoral dissertation, Department of Sociology, University of Oregon.

Teas, R.K. (1980), "Empirical Tests of Linkages Proposed in the Walker, Churchill and Ford Model of Sales Force Motivation and Performance," *Journal of the Academy of Marketing Science,* 8 (Winter/Spring), 58–72.

Teas, R.K. (1981a), "A Test of a Model of Department Store Salespeople's Job Satisfaction," *Journal of Retailing,* 57 (Spring), 3–25.

Teas, R.K. (1981b), "An Empirical Test of Models of Salespersons' Job Expectancy and Instrumentality Perceptions," *Journal of Marketing Research,* 18 (May), 209–226.

Teas, R.K. (1981c), "Selling Task Characteristics and the Job Satisfaction of Industrial Salespeople," *Journal of Personal Selling and Sales Management,* 1 (Spring/Summer), 18–26.

Teas, R.K. (1982), "Performance-Reward Instrumentalities and the Motivation of Retail Salespeople," *Journal of Retailing,* 58 (Fall), 4–26.

Teas, R.K. (1983), "Supervisory Behavior, Role Stress, and the Job Satisfaction of Industrial Salespeople," *Journal of Marketing Research,* 20 (February), 84–91.

Teas, R.K., J. Wacker, and R.E. Hughes (1979), "Path Analysis of Causes and Consequences of Salespeople's Perceptions of Role Clarity," *Journal of Marketing Research,* 16 (August), 355–369.

Tobolski, F.P. and W.A. Kerr (1952), "Predictive Value of the Empathy Test in Automobile Salesmanship," *Journal of Applied Psychology,* 36 (October), 310–311.

Tosdal, H.R. (1953), "How to Design the Salesman's Compensation Plan," *Harvard Business Review,* 31 (September–October), 61–70.

Tosi, H.L. (1966), "The Effects of Expectation Levels and Role Consensus on the Buyer-Seller Dyad," *Journal of Business,* 39 (October), 516–529.

Tyagi, P.K. (1980), "Influence of Organizational Climate on Salespeople's Valence for Intrinsic and Extrinsic Job Outcomes," in 1980 AMA Educators' Conference *Proceedings,* R.P. Bagozzi et al., eds. (Chicago: American Marketing Association), 234–237.

Tyagi, P.K. (1982), "Perceived Organizational Climate and the Process of Salesperson Motivation," *Journal of Marketing Research,* 14 (May), 240–254.

Valecha, G.K. (1975), "Abbreviated 11-Item Rotter IE Scale," in *Measures of Social Psychological Attitudes,* J.P. Robinson and P.R. Shaver, eds. (Ann Arbor, MI: Institute for Social Research).

Vroom, V. (1963), *Some Personality Determinants of the Effects of Participation* (Englewood Cliffs, NJ: Prentice-Hall).

Vroom, V. (1964), *Work and Motivation* (New York: Wiley).

Walker, O.C., G.A. Churchill, and N.M. Ford (1972), "Reactions to Role Conflict: The Case of the Industrial Salesman," *Journal of Business Administration,* 3 (Spring), 25–36.

Walker, O.C., G.A. Churchill, and N.M. Ford (1975), "Organizational Determinants of the Industrial Salesman's Role Conflict and Ambiguity," *Journal of Marketing,* 30 (January), 32–39.

Walker, O.C., G.A. Churchill, and N.M. Ford (1977), "Motivation and Performance in Industrial Selling: Present Knowledge and Needed Research, *Journal of Marketing Research,* 14 (May), 156–168.

Walker, O.C., G.A. Churchill, and N.M. Ford (1979), "Where Do We Go from Here? Selected Conceptual and Empirical Issues Concerning the Motivation and Performance of the Industrial Sales Force," in *Critical Issues in Sales Management: State-of-the-Art and Future Research Needs,* G. Albaum and G.A. Churchill, eds. (Eugene, OR: University of Oregon Press), 10–75.

Weaver, C.N. (1969), "An Empirical Study to Aid in the Selection of Retail Salesclerks," *Journal of Retailing,* 45 (Fall), 22–26.

Weiss, D.J., R.V. Davis, G.W. England, and L.H. Lofquest (1969), *Manual for Minnesota Studies in Vocational Rehabilitation XXII* (Minneapolis: Industrial Relations Research Center).

Weitz, B.A. (1978), "Relationship Between Salesperson Performance and the Understanding of Customer Decision Making," *Journal of Marketing Research,* 15 (November), 501–516.

Weitz, B.A. (1979), "A Critical Review of Personal Selling Research: The Need for Contingency Approaches," in *Critical Issues in Sales Management: State-of-the-Art and Future Research Needs,* G. Albaum and G.A. Churchill, eds. (Eugene, OR: University of Oregon).

Wilson, D.T. and L. Bozinoff (1980), "Role Theory and Buying-Selling Negotiations: A Critical Review," in *1980 AMA Educators' Conference Proceedings,* R.P. Bagozzi et al., eds. (Chicago: American Marketing Association), 118–121.

Winer, L. (1973), "The Effect of Product Sales Force Productivity," *Journal of Marketing Research,* 10 (May), 180–183.

Witkin, A.A. (1956), "Differential Interest Patterns in Salesmen," *Journal of Applied Psychology,* 40 (October), 338–340.

Zdep, S.M. and H.B. Weaver (1967), "The Graphoanalytic Approach to Selecting Life Insurance Salesmen," *Journal of Applied Psychology,* 51 (June), 295–299.

Zelkowitz, R. (1975), "The Construction and Validation of a Measure of Vocational Maturity for Adult Males," unpublished Ph.D. dissertation, Department of Psychology, Columbia University.

Author Index

Aaker, A., 46, 47, 55, 108, 127
Albaum, G., 10, 16, 78, 79
Alutto, J.A., 117
Auld, H.D., 119, 129
Austin, R.L., 9, 10, 73

Baehr, M.E., 11, 75
Bagozzi, R.P., 15, 45, 46, 47, 53, 55, 56, 83, 107, 108, 109, 126, 127, 128
Baier, D., 21, 84
Barry, T.E., 57
Becherer, R.C., 35, 47, 94, 114
Behrman, D.N., 46, 54, 55, 111, 129
Belasco, J.A., 33
Bellenger, D.N., 34, 38, 97
Bennett, P.D., 29
Berkowitz, E.N., 46, 55, 110, 128
Berry, B.A., 105, 122
Berry, L., 23
Bigoness, W.J., 46, 54
Borgatta, E.F., 82, 126, 128
Borys, R.H., 40, 46, 48, 55, 103, 112, 129
Brown, S.H., 20, 21, 86
Burke, R.J., 103, 110
Burstiner, I., 23
Busch, P., 40, 41, 46, 49, 55, 102, 103, 108, 110, 112, 127, 129
Bush, R.F., 40, 46, 55, 102, 103, 108, 112, 127, 129

Campbell, J.P., 31, 53
Chonko, L.B., 41, 103
Churchill, G.A., 2, 5, 6, 20, 23, 30, 33, 34, 40, 41, 45, 46, 47, 48, 49, 89, 91, 101, 106, 115, 129

Clarke, W.V., 19, 20, 21, 84
Claxton, J.D., 23
Collins, B.E., 126
Collins, R.H., 20, 23
Connolly, T., 31
Cotham, J.C., III, 23, 24, 87, 88
Cravens, D.W., 55, 56, 130
Crissy, W.J.E., 57
Cunningham, W.H., 49

Darmon, R.Y., 30, 119
Day, R.L., 29
Dessler, G., 32, 94, 104, 112
Deutscher, T., 23
Dillard, J.F., 31
Donnelly, J.H., 46, 47, 103, 105, 109, 110, 122, 127
Doyle, S.X., 33, 34, 92
Dubinsky, A.J., 33, 35, 40, 41, 46, 47, 48, 53, 55, 57, 100, 104, 109, 111, 112, 116, 128, 129, 130
Dugan, R.D., 21, 84
Duncan, O.D., 109, 128
Dunham, R.B., 115
Dunnette, M.D., 11, 15, 16, 79
Durand, R.M., 9, 11

Einhorn, H.J., 31
English, W.D., 49
Evans, F.B., 19, 23, 85

Farley, J.U., 30
Finn, D.W., 55, 56
Fischer, P.M., 47
Ford, N.M., 2, 5, 6, 30, 33, 34, 40, 41, 45, 46, 47, 48, 49, 89, 91, 101, 107, 129

About the Authors

James M. Comer is currently an associate professor of marketing at the University of Cincinnati. Prior to earning his doctorate from Northwestern University, he was a sales representative and manager with E.I. DuPont de Nemours. He has published articles on sales management in the *Journal of Marketing, Journal of Marketing Research, Journal of Personal Selling and Sales Management,* and *Decision Sciences.* In addition to being a sales management consultant, he is a regular participant and contributor to the Proceedings of the American Marketing Association and the Institute of Management Sciences. He is a member of the American Marketing Association, the Institute of Management Sciences, and the Sales and Marketing Executives Club.

Alan J. Dubinsky is a visiting associate professor of marketing in the School of Management at the University of Minnesota, and has served on the faculties of Southern Methodist University and University of Kentucky. He received his B.S.B., M.B.A., and Ph.D. from the University of Minnesota. Prior to pursuing graduate work, he was a territory manager for Burroughs Corporation. His publications have appeared in *Journal of Retailing, Journal of Advertising, Industrial Marketing Management, California Management Review, MSU Business Topics, Business Horizons, Journal of Personal Selling and Sales Management, Journal of Purchasing and Materials Management, Psychological Reports, Journal of Risk and Insurance, European Journal of Management, Journal of Consumer Marketing, Psychology and Marketing,* and *Journal of the Academy of Marketing Science.* He is the author of a book titled *Sales Training: An Analysis of Field Sales Techniques* (UMI Research Press). He is on the Editorial Board of the *Journal of Personal Selling and Sales Management.* In addition, he conducts professional development seminars for industry that focus on general marketing management and selling and sales management.